UNITED
STATES
SOCIALIST
REPUBLIC™

To Nancy
Best Wishes
Hugo

UNITED STATES SOCIALIST REPUBLIC™

*The Liberal / Marxist Machine and
The Men, Method and Means to
Fundamentally Transform America*

H. G. GOERNER

Charleston, SC
www.PalmettoPublishing.com

***U.nited S.tates S.ocialist R.epublic*™**

Hardcover: 978-1-64990-416-4
Paperback: 978-1-64111-284-0
eBook: 978-1-64111-004-4

Acknowledgements

For my brother Jim and his wife Elaine, who gave me what I needed most; love.

For Dan, the best friend a man could ever have.

For Tom, who helped me stay sane.

For Dr. Thomas Sowell, an intellectual giant without whom I would never have been able to make sense of all this chaos.

For Major Stephen Coughlin (ret.) a former intelligence analyst at the Pentagon, who pointed out the realities of the battle we are in for the future of America.

Finally, I gratefully acknowledge Senator Ted Cruz for inspiring me to get involved.

In late April 2016, I was asked to attend a fundraiser in Santa Barbara, Ca. for Senator Cruz and assist with some of the logistical matters. Before the Senator was due to arrive his driver called and asked me to escort their vehicle to the property, and I happily obliged. At this dinner, I was able to sit quietly near the Senator's table while they dined. It was then, as I listened to his words during those several minutes, that I came away with what I perceived to be true greatness. Politically, intellectually and morally, Senator Cruz stood out, and had a clear vision of what America IS. I witnessed his brilliant command of concepts within the Constitution and all its complexities, and what he wanted for all Americans.

I will never ever forget those 30 minutes for as long as I live. It was at those very moments that my life had a new direction. He inspired me to get involved and do all that I could to keep our America...Ours.

We now stand on the precipice. The Liberal / Marxist Machine will take America and Transform it...if we allow them. They want to burn it down, and start over. They want to turn our America into THEIR America.

Senator Cruz knows all too well, what that America would look like.

This book is dedicated to the remembrance of my dear friend and mentor, Neal Andrews, who patiently prodded me and quietly supported my attempts to turn my views into words. With a lifetime of conservative values expressed by him through contributions at the national, regional, and local levels, the inspiration and insight he provided are needed now more than ever.

Table of Contents

Preface

It was not until I began to get a fuller understanding of what was behind all this mayhem and rioting in our cities over the last year that I actually put serious thought to writing about it.

A very good friend of mine, Major Stephen Coughlin (ret.), took the time to explain these issues in a reality-based manner. These folks we see protesting, rioting. They are creating mayhem, and are not, by any means, your average everyday citizens or civil rights protesters. These are Specialists. Specialists in creating doubt, division, and the appearance of wrongdoing and impropriety on the part of all red-blooded American patriots who are resisting the country's lurch toward liberalism, and who, for some reason, are now anathema to contemporary American values and culture.

The terms "Racist" "Nationalist" and "cultural oppression" have seeped into the American dialogue for so long, and are now so deeply imbedded, there is no clear way of turning back. We are past the point of no return. The flood gates have opened fully; and we, my fellow citizens, are under water. These specialists are drowning our nation in political correctness; changing not only what we see in our news, but much of how and where public opinion is shaped.

Major Coughlin made one point that hit me particularly hard. It took my breath away, and it still rings in my ears: "These folks we see protesting, rioting, creating mayhem, are the front of the crowd. There are a huge number of protagonists in this scenario who are hidden."

Major Coughlin referred to them all as Marxists. These are American-born NEO-MARXISTS!! These Marxists hide under the banner of "Good Little Liberals." Well mannered Democrats. So polite. They hide under a patriotic banner, and call themselves Progressives, or Liberals. But I believe them to be part of a Machine; what I will refer to here as the Liberal/Marxist Machine.

Please bear in mind...These Liberal / Marxists I refer to are nothing like the Liberals of old. Certainly nothing at all like the JFK's, nor the RFK's, or even the FDR's. Those sorts of patriotic Liberals have long since disappeared into the PC abyss. We are now faced with a more revolutionary Liberal. Part of a human machine, that feels nothing but shame for the country they live in, and want to transform.

A large, stealthy Machine in this country has come out of hiding, and there are literally hundreds of elected officials and government insiders that are part of this machine, who would sell America out; who would compromise the foundation of our democracy, for a seat at the head of the global table of power.

The sad part is, that these supposedly average everyday folks we see on the news rioting in our cities, smashing store windows and looting businesses with graffiti phrases like "Eat the Rich," they are being swayed by a leftist leadership that has already bought into this Marxist Dialectic. The rioters have bought in, but they may have no clue about the end game. They have no conception of what can be lost. Should real Marxist ideology and political socialism get a firm foothold, America will never, ever be the same. What's more: every single person on the planet can eventually kiss their individual self-determination. . . Good Bye.

For centuries people around the world have understood that life is largely a series of trade-offs, and we have laws in this country to address and remedy these disparities and injustices. We have lived with these inequities and disparities, and accepted them, and we all have moved forward. I am not suggesting that Americans should not be open to change. Indeed, we are a nation of innovators who have transformed the world through technology, international development, and global commerce. But there are inherent trade-offs in the capitalist American democratic system. And virtually all citizens say they want equality. Yet all of us...every single one of us, would trade our lives in a moment, for one of privilege and wealth.

If you say you wouldn't, you're a liar.

Introduction

When I began this writing this reveal, I knew what I wanted to say; how I was going to lay it all out by connecting the dots. But I never expected to reveal to myself and to those around me a much bigger and more dangerous set of truths, which largely explain the state of our beloved country today.

The information compiled as the basis for this text is not just a gaggle of interesting points. It is, in the end, an uncomfortable announcement to my fellow citizens that America as we know and love her, is under attack by an anarchist Marxist mob. An insurrection mounted over decades, which is culminating now. As you read on, bear in mind that I have been guided by my life experience, my own curiosity, my research, and a few very good people who took the time to point me in the right direction.

A truly great man I knew and loved passed away just over one year ago. Neal Andrews was the mayor of my town, an incredibly intelligent man—a member of MENSA—and an authentic, grounded and humble person. Above all, Neal was a student of political history and could virtually see the future of things. He could read the signs that most of us would dismiss. And he fully appreciated what the great Thomas Sowell has professed: that life will always be a series of trade-offs.

Neal and I would get together almost every Sunday evening – for two full years until his passing—and discuss current events and the urgent issues of our time. The thing he and I discussed most often was the economic state of California. Many Californians will argue themselves Blue over this

Fact-- The State of California is insolvent. The state's unfunded liabilities add up to almost a Trillion dollars. Yes, that is "one-thousand billion dollars" in liabilities not covered. Needless to say, in the world fiscal fitness, this is unsustainable. Of this there is no doubt. Without political posturing or financial wrangling, Neal and I concluded that bankruptcy protection is inevitable for the Golden State. And—even before COVID-19—I shared my assumptions and calculations with friends, not with any pride of clairvoyance, but with a sense of frustration and dread, as they confirmed my thinking with concrete examples. Let me share just one.

In 2018 in a conversation with a very sharp friend of mine with an Ivy League education, I heard that our local government retirement expenditures were in the billions of dollars and growing. I understood this to be normal, and just the way municipalities need to operate. Until we talked about "retirement spiking." The more I learned, the more concerned I became. So, I started to dig. And man, did I get my eyes opened. Just one manager in our local government who had recently retired from the health department after nineteen years would be receiving a monthly pension of $19,000 per month. Forever. This despite the fact that her regular salary was about half that amount. But by "cashing out" unused sick and vacation time in the last three pay periods of her tenure, she could "spike" her monthly pension—in perpetuity—and it was completely legal. This pension liability amounts to $228,000 per year, plus health insurance. And this person was not in an executive leadership position; just one of hundreds in middle management who could take the first $10,000 per month to live on, put the other $9,000 into savings, and in less than ten years, would have more than $1 million dollars in their savings account. All covered by us, taxpayers.

If you want to experience an epiphany, take a look at your local city or county pension funds. The person I'm referencing is just one of tens of thousands on the pension payroll, with no end in sight. And with the 2018 total unfunded liabilities for California pegged at 883 Billion dollars, the actuary takes it much higher—about 1.5 Trillion dollars—leading all states in the nation, with Illinois running a fairly close second, and thirty three more states in line.[1]

When you take a closer look at the fiscal realities of these states you see that most all are run by Democrats. Or at least that is their party affiliation. But I wrote this book in part to let people know that they, in fact, are NOT Democrats in the traditional sense or understanding. They are a newer breed. They claim they are for the little guy who struggles, the homeless, the poor, and the disenfranchised. Good Grief! Just once I wish these new liberals could tell the truth.

Right now in America, approximately fifty percent of the citizenry is being supported by our government in one way or another. Of course, this is not shared too widely in polite dinner conversations, but it's the other fifty percent that pay the bills.[2]

That is socialism. That's the U.S.S.R.- The United States Socialist Republic.

How can anything be more fair and equal? The successful class covers the costs of the ever-expanding welfare class. We think our tax dollars will be invested wisely and that "a high tide lifts all boats." Until... we find out that American Marxists want even more. Much more indeed.

What more do they want? And why are they willing to break the rules in order to get it?

A New American System. A so-called "Fundamental Transformation" of what we now have. And you know what would be funny if it weren't so infuriating? If we ask them what they would put in the place of our current capitalist democracy—the most successful nation in the world history—they get this strange look on their face and start to scratch their heads. They cannot articulate the What or the Who or the How to make this

1 California Policy Center, *California's State and Local Liabilities Total $1.5 Trillion*; Joffe and Ring. (January 3, 2019) *www californiapolicycenter.org*. https://californiapolicycenter.org/californias-state-and-local-liabilities-total-1-5-trillion-2/

2 Forbes magazine; *Romney was wrong about the 47 percent, the problem is much worse.* Jeffrey Dorfman (December 19, 2013). *www.Forbes.com.* https://www.forbes.com/sites/jeffreydorfman/2013/12/19/romney-was-wrong-about-the-47-percent-the-problem-is-much-worse/#7791266117fa

supposed transformation work. No leadership. No foundation for systematic alterations. No new agencies that can provide resources or services to the masses more efficiently or effectively. They simply want to transform our current system to a more equitable and fair society. Well, that is what we all want. But they see the path to get there very differently than you or me. Because the Utopia they see is in the clouds, and they are not willing to sacrifice anything of substance to achieve meaningful change. They feel they are entitled to a just, fair and equitable society. Now. The Constitution tells them so.

No Karen...keep reading.

If we are to give our consent to be governed, we will need to be willing to accept being governed. We are not all geniuses, so there are inevitably going to be some trade-offs. If you drive down the highway drunk and hurt or kill someone in a crash, be prepared to trade a little of your freedom for the 'liberty' to flaunt the law.

For the sake of argument, let us suppose that the current incarnation of the Black Lives Matter movement is actually trying to accomplish what we would hope they are: Improve the plight of disadvantaged African-Americans in this great country, and black community at large. As good people do, we donate to their cause. And we receive a confirmation of our donation. And the movement continues on to create more and better opportunities, and the world becomes a better place. However, some information has come out that might just throw a wrench into the works. It might even shake the foundations of race equity and advocacy. Huge amounts of money donated to BLM never make it to the destination. That's right. Millions of dollars intended to support community action and coordination goes to a third party. When we donate to BLM through a link online, and recognize that the organization lacks the capacity to manage these funds, we are not surprised that an organization, Thousand Currents, is contracted to manage the donations to finance Black Lives Matter. But here is the wrench: Thousand Currents is managed by former Weather Underground operative and domestic terrorist Susan Rosenberg...or at least she was the Vice Chair of record until recently. Now it appears she has gone into hiding and information about her position on the Board of Directors on the company website deleted.[3]

So, what is the connection between a fringe group of anarchist extremists from the 1970s known as the Weather Underground and the intense conflict and rioting we see resulting from the Black Lives Matter movement? I will show in the pages that follow that a direct line can be drawn between the Marxist extremism that fueled domestic terrorist attacks decades ago, up through the perversion of our schools and other institutions, to the social upheaval and violence we see today.

It appears that large portions of Marxists in America want to destroy statues and other likenesses that remind us of our country's history. Whether it is Confederate generals and flags to be torn down, or central historical figures like President Andrew Jackson removed from currency, the contemporary Liberal/Marxist Machine is up and running. They do not want citizens to have to be 'confronted" with the mistakes and clashes of the last three centuries. They call for tearing down statues of religious, political, and social leaders of years past with the resolution that "these mistakes shall never be repeated."

Unfortunately, when we ignore or refuse to even acknowledge our past, we are ensuring quite the opposite. It will sneak up on us quietly and bite us right in the ass. We should know by now that we ignore and rewrite history at our own peril. ANYONE, no matter how intelligent or experienced they may be, cannot ignore the mistakes of their past. Even Einstein had an eraser.

It is unbelievably short-sighted and ignorant—bordering on insanity—that huge swaths of America have been mobilized into tearing down statues that commemorate past victories and losses, past heroes and sacrifices made to build the United States we have inherited today. Next, these folks will demand that no one make mention of past atrocities of humankind, perpetrated by, and suffered upon, our forebears. The mere mentioning of

---

3 Capital Research Center, InfluenceWatch.org, (2020); Susan Rosenberg, Weather Underground and Thousand Currents. https//www.influencewatch.org/person/susan-rosenberg/

the people or events may be considered off limits—censored to be politically correct.

If you have never seen or heard the following quote, it is high time you did.

"The best way to take control over a people and control them utterly, is to take a little of their freedom at a time, to erode rights by a thousand tiny and almost imperceptible reductions. In this way, the people will not see those rights and freedoms being removed until past the point at which these changes cannot be reversed."[4] Although this quote is from a piece of fiction, it has recently gained traction online in contemporary political discourse, precisely because it rings true to so many who feel the threat of encroaching socialist influence and undermining of our freedoms.

My fellow citizens, I submit to you that a reckoning is indeed upon us, but it is not the one that we are told is at hand. We must come to terms with a vast, sophisticated Liberal/Marxist Machine that has been unleashed within our country. Clear-eyed, long term decisions must be made before even greater losses of individual freedoms are forfeited.

The Machine refuses to acknowledge the abundance of Fairness under the Rule of Law in America. It refuses to acknowledge the Equality of Opportunity that abounds for everyone who comes here. In addition, the people running this Machine seem to think that, Equity of Outcome should be mandatory. Be that as it may, I have to admit... I cannot wait for these Marxists to discover that ultimately, they too, would wind up being controlled by the very machine they built.

So the choice is now before all of us; whether to buy in to the promises of the new Marxist America-- the United States Socialist Republic, or to resist the gradual elimination of our individual rights and freedoms, and to organize against the social revolution that is now a very real threat we all face. To understand how I perceive this threat, please read on.

---

4 *Willfully Ignorant*, by Pat Miller. (2014) fiction. WestBow Press.

Insidious Beginnings

About ten years ago I was researching the background of radical activist Bill Ayers and how he had been traveling around the United States speaking to teachers during their union meetings about American Anti-Imperialism, and I came across this name: **Robert Muller.**[5] He was the quiet, unassuming United Nations moral provocateur. "No War, No Poverty, No Hunger" was his clarion call. And as we will see in the final chapter, Muller had a profound erosive effect on the concept of American exceptionalism, cultivating support for one world governance within government circles, and, perhaps unwittingly, helped light the fuse for the social unrest we see exploding today.

In the 1960s, Bill Ayers was the radical domestic terrorist who spawned the Weather Underground and who managed to walk free after facing murder charges. Soon after beating the rap, he went into hiding for almost dozen years, only to resurface in New York City at Bank Street College in 1984.[6] Before we go further, let me share a few thoughts to link contemporary protests and Marxist radicalism with the insidious progression of Bill Ayers from a leader in bombing the NYC Police Department and U.S.

---

5 Robert Muller, *Appeal to All Leaders of Nations,* (September 200). Ideas and Dreams for a Better World; RobertMuller.com; http://robertmuller.org/lead/p01.html

6 Seeking Educational Excellence (SEE), *Bill Ayers- biography*, (2020). https://seekingeducationalexcellence.org/william-ayers/

Capitol decades ago, to a leader in shaping the core beliefs of our youth over the last thirty-five years.

Where is the frustration, the sense of entitlement, and the disconnect with American traditions and social order among our millennial generation coming from? They must be getting this from somewhere. They've got to be taught this, right? That is correct. And the teacher of our teachers is Bill Ayers. How do I know this?

1. Ayers received a Masters degree from Bank Street College in "Early Childhood Education" 1984
2. Ayers received another Masters degree from Columbia University "Early Childhood Education" 1987
3. Ayers then received a PhD in Education from Columbia University "Curriculum and Education" 1987

To clearly view today's protests and riots, we need to look back and appreciate the nexus between Ayers's radical pedigree, and the relationships which explain his role in shaping the present-day assault on American institutions, which are framed as a fight against American imperialism. This assault shapes not only American politics, but, I submit, limits American progress.

RADICALISM GOES TO SCHOOL

It was with the formation of the Weather Underground in the 1960s that Bill Ayers would begin his terrorizing and physical assault on what he believed to be the institutions of American government imperialism and also those persons in positions of authority. He started a campaign of bombing public buildings in the late 1960s and was a leader of the SDS: Students for a Democratic Society. During those bombings, a police officer was killed, and so were a close friend and the girlfriend of Ayers. But due to

FBI mishandling of the case, Ayers walked free, and later bragged about it to the press. "Guilty as sin. Free as a Bird. I Love America."[7]

In 1974 Ayers published the book "Prairie Fire: The Politics of Revolutionary Anti-Imperialism," in collaboration with other members of the Weather Underground organization.[8] The best way for anyone to understand its simple yet destructive message can be explained in the following article, *Prairie Fire in the Classroom: Bill Ayers's Bloodless Revolution* by William M. Briggs (2018)[9]. Recognize, however, that Bill Ayers is merely a continuance of a deeper and much longer dissent in the American social experiment that started around 1905. The extended excerpt here from Mr. Briggs' article will start to clear the path for us to see the insidious nature of Ayers's assault. The article illuminates the modern shakedown of Traditional Americanism. And shakedown, in my opinion, is the perfect word to describe the assault we are witnessing on America today. It is practically mass coercion, and the young adults rioting today can be seen as the toxic fruits of Ayers's many years of investment in fundamental social engineering.

> Bill Ayers 2006 speech to the World Economic Forum in Caracas, Venezuela
> *"We share the belief that education is the motor-force of Revolution"*

> Glenn E Singleton, 2006.
> *"John Dewey suggested that schools must be the engine for Social Transformation"*

---

7 National Review. "Guilty as sin. Free as a Bird." Jay Nordlinger (August 28, 2008) www.nationalreview.com https://www.nationalreview.com/corner/guilty-sin-free-bird-jay-nordlinger/

8 **PRAIRIE FIRE: The Politics of Revolutionary Anti-Imperialism** The Political Statement of the Weather Underground, May 1974 (reprint edition, PDF), Dohrn, Ayers. From Students for a Democratic Society – SDS, Weatherman/Weather Underground Organization (2020); https://www.sds-1960s.org/PrairieFire-reprint.pdf

9 Briggs, WM, *Prairie Fire in the Classroom: Bill Ayers's Bloodless Revolution*, (March 22, 2018) https://wmbriggs.com/post/24136/

Vladimir Lenin. circa 1918. .
> *"Give me four years to teach the children, and the seed I have sewn will never be uprooted"*

As Briggs wrote in 2018:

> *. . . And then there was Bill Ayers. While the 2008 McCain-Palin Campaign briefly [and ineptly] focused on Ayer's days as a domestic terrorist with the Weather Underground, it failed to discuss Ayer's work in education during the past several decades. It was that work, and not Ayer's terrorist past, that attracted Obama to the former terrorist.*

> *Obama worked with Ayers on the Chicago Annenberg Challenge and served with Ayers on the board of the leftist Woods Fund from 1998 until 2001. . . According to Ayers in "Public Enemy: Confessions of an American Dissident" [2013], the Woods Fund "supported community organizing." Members of the Weather Underground called themselves "Community organizers," as did Obama.*

> *Obama provided praise for Ayer's book A Kind and Just Parent in 1997. Ayers returned the favor the following year in Teaching for Social Justice when he included Obama's Dreams From My Father from a list of books that are "resources for teaching for change."*

> *Obama and Ayers even appeared together on academic panels, including one organized by Michelle Obama to discuss the juvenile justice system as an area of mutual concern.*

> *The Weather Underground's interest in education was evident even when they were planning a violent revolution in the United*

States. "We believe that radical teachers should work in schools in working class neighborhoods, in community or junior colleges" Ayers, et al, wrote in Prairie Fire, their 1974 political manifesto. "Radicalizing our teachers, organizing the parents, teach and encourage your students." Ayer's opinion about radicalizing teachers was unchanged four decades after Prairie Fire. "Revolutionaries want to change the world, of course, and teachers, it turns out, want to change the world too – typically one child at a time," he wrote in Public Enemy. "It wasn't as much as a reach as you might imagine."

So how, would these radicalized teachers change the world? Ayers and his wife, Bernadine Dohrn a Weather Underground comrade, offer an answer to that question in "Race Course Against White Supremacy" 2009. "If you want fundamental change, tie your fate to the most oppressed." The title of their book makes it clear who they consider the oppressed and who they consider the oppressors. The "Fundamental change" [or "Fundamental Transformation" as Obama put it in 2008] they desire is more socialism in this country.

What is going on here? I believe Ayers and his fellow radical teachers have succeeded in getting a "Prairie Fire" curriculum in our nation's classrooms. As Ayers and Dohrn noted in "Race Course against White Supremacy," they're promoting this fundamental change by tying their fate to the "most oppressed," i.e., minorities. It's a brilliant strategy since opposing that change opens one up to being called a racist. The promotion of fundamental change is even taking place in a deep Red state like Kansas. The February 2, 2014 issue of my hometown newspaper, the Lawrence Journal-World included an article about Leidene King of the San Francisco-based PEG. . . Pacific Educational Group presenting a two-day program entitled "Beyond Diversity: An

*Introduction to Courageous Conversations and a Foundation
for Deinstitutionalizing Racism and Eliminating Racial
Achievement Disparities."*

*"Courageous conversations" is based on a book by Glen E.
Singleton, PEG CEO and Curtis Linton. The program is
rooted in a discipline known as CRT. . . Critical Race Theory.
What is CRT? The UCLA School of Public Affairs answers
that question. . .*

*CRT recognizes that racism is ingrained in the fabric and the
system of American society. The individual racist need not exist to note the institutional racism is pervasive in the dominant
culture. This is the analytical lens that CRT uses in examining existing power structures. CRT identifies that these power
structures are based on white supremacy, which perpetuates the
marginalization of people of color. CRT also rejects the traditions of liberalism and meritocracy. Legal discourse says that the
law is neutral and colorblind, however, CRT challenges this legal
"Truth" by examining liberalism and meritocracy as a vehicle for
self-interest, power, and privilege.*

*According to Robert Holland of the Lexington Institute, CRT
"Is a radical academic doctrine that gained currency in elite U.
S. law schools in the 1980s and 1990s, and has more recently
taken hold with multi-culturalism advocates in teacher-training
instructions." "One of the progenitors of CRT, the late Derrick
Bell, a Harvard University professor, berated liberal civil-rights
scholars for their championship of a colorblind society." Holland
continued, "Like many of his allies, he relied largely on narrative
and anecdote to advance his arguments and argued for sweeping
societal transformation generated more by political organizing
than rights-based legal remedies.*

Interestingly, Bell was one of Obama's law professors at Harvard. When Obama was a lecturer at the University of Chicago Law School, one of the courses he taught was a seminar entitled "Current Issues on Racism and Law." Bell was one of the writers Obama required his students to read. In an interview prior to his death, Bell discussed the Marxist foundation of CRT. As of 2009, Bell served as a sponsor of New Politics; a magazine predominately staffed and run my members of the DSA. Democratic Socialists of America.

The Briggs' article points out how the Liberal Machine seems to just gather around the water cooler at every corner in America and expound on how pervasive racism and oppression is in this county. He suggests that there are communities and organizations that get encouraged by the discussion, and then, we end up seeing the Democratic Socialists of America, various Socialist organizations and the Democratic Liberal/Marxist currency of protest being passed around among us all. It seems the culture of protest is now widespread, even if reason is not. Unfortunately, the results are toxic, and the youngest minds get affected by the hyperbole the most.

The Democratic Socialist "solution" catches on with our idealistic young because they haven't experienced it, and because they believe in the promises without critical examination of the alternatives. The mainstream media plugs in the narrative (even when the results are bad for the individual sovereignty) and the whole thing goes viral. The next thing we see are riots and youngsters at our colleges violently disrupting discourse with destruction and/or protests. As Briggs observed, it is CRT "Critical Race Theory" that is taught in our colleges and this school of thought lends credence and momentum to what we are seeing today with the nearly universal use of the slur "Racist" to attack even well-considered positions that challenge the assumptions, if we disagree with the theory, or disagree even a little. .

Our children see the world through the lenses of idealism, passion, and fear. They rise up in small groups and attempt to bring about change. All along the way, the only thing getting any media coverage is the fear and concern; fear about global warming, race-based discrimination, and corporate domination. As observers, the adults sympathize and genuinely feel concern. But in the end, nothing is moved. Nothing is changed. The only real effects are the ones the adults put on paper and sanction with legislation. Is it just me, or do these protests and riots seem to have only one thing in common? Virtually no one over the age of forty.

It's that innocence, passion and idealism that Ayers sought to exploit. Unfortunately for us all, that innocence doesn't get replaced with experience, wisdom and understanding until it's too late. Young people today are frustrated. But they have no solutions, only complaints. And this is to be expected, as the logical extension of Ayers's approach to 'transformation/revolution.'

Here's the kicker: the DSA—the Democratic Socialists of America—has been at work since 1982. The organization has its roots in the Socialist Party of America (1901), in which a prominent American participated between 1920 and 1949. His name was Norman Thomas, and he was a perpetual candidate for the Office of the Presidency. He ran for the office six times and during one campaign in 1936 he gained one million votes. That's a heck of a lot of Liberal/Marxists voters and votes in a country with a population of slightly over 100 million. In that 1936 Presidential election, barely 49 million votes were cast. That shows that the Socialist movement was being heard and was not going away easily, if at all.

Here is one statement that some attribute to Norman Thomas that greatly concerns me

"Americans will never knowingly adopt Socialism. But eventually, under the name Liberalism, the American people will adopt every fragment of the socialist program. . . and they won't even know how it happened."[10]

10 The Daily Herald – Chicago *Socialism will creep up on us* (November 12, 2011) - https://www.dailyherald.com/article/20111112/discuss/711129957/

Since at least the 1940s, this indirect approach to change seems to be working. Inch by inch, mile by mile, and body by body, we see it in contemporary America. And there are several well-funded players that are moving the country in this direction, about whom the reader should be concerned.

Bill Ayers is the Modern Socialist/Anarchist that despises America and all its Imperialist Sins. But stunning in its absence and born of Ayers's hubris and idealistic endeavor is the fact that he does not consider the complex realities or the actual logistics of his revolution. Ayers's vision is actually moving closer to reality without the requisite plans for true democratic governance.

It's pure insanity.

Here, allow me to be more bold. Ayers is extremely dangerous! And when I say dangerous, it is not in the vein of a serial killer, the DC shooter or a Folsom prison murderer. He is not pathological in that sense; not anti-social in behavior. Ayers is actually very erudite and social. Very likeable, in that he puts a great deal of effort into being so.

But I contend that Ayers is a hundred times more dangerous than was Norman Thomas, and even in the scope of anarchists with a penchant for destruction and mayhem. Here is the reality of his sophistication of destruction: he is going after our most precious, our most wonderful, our most loved; **Our Children**. He sees them not as the future of the great American melting pot, but as a resource for his Liberal/Marxist plan; for his Bloodless Revolution.

The Nonsense Equation

When I assert that Ayers is extremely dangerous, I actually say that with a combination anxiety and a bit of humor. Let me explain.

Ayers, with all that he achieved academically, might lead you to believe his desire for Revolution was anti-social, and, more importantly, pathological. But actually, it's quite the opposite. Any committed revolutionary, with all that he could muster, would seek out avenues, political confederates and most importantly, his adversaries. First, avenues must be considered to wage a campaign without exposure. Second, confederates must be identified and enlisted who will take part and sacrifice. And thirdly, as with any revolution, adversaries must be identified, and ultimately, eliminated.

These particular elements of a revolution are critical to the success of the undertaking. And here is the quandary I came across in my research. Ayers never put a great deal of thought into these elements. The How, the Team, and the Opposition. These predict the Results. This is the part that stunned me: He failed to anticipate the likely results.

FBI informant Larry Grathwohl was interviewed in a documentary "No Place to Hide: The Strategy and Tactics of Terrorism" after successfully infiltrating Ayers's organization[11]. He was stunned by the lack of effective post-revolution planning, and the responsibilities of the socialist

---

11 HBO Entertainment. (1982) documentary *"No Place to Hide: The Strategy and Tactics of Terrorism"* by Western Goals Foundation; uploaded November 2, 2010. https://archive.org/details/NoPlaceToHide-TerrorismDocumentary

leadership in meeting the needs of 250 million people. But this is just a fragment of the nonsense.

Grathwohl was able to discuss the logistics of the coup with Bill Ayers, but never could come to grips with the fact that Ayers really had no idea, nor had he contemplated the actions required to fulfill his vision. So, what I mean by "very dangerous," is there are multiple aspects to the Ayers threat. He planned with others to have "re-education camps" for those who resist, and apparently had no compunction about killing dissenters who might refuse his new order. The FBI agent discusses this with Ayers, and it is the way he so matter-of-factly considered it an errand which is so striking. Like taking out the trash.[12]

FBI informant Grathwohl responds to questions about Ayers and gives his account of Ayer's re-education tactics in a recorded interview. The chilling precept of Bill Ayers' total lack of any reality-based understanding of how an actual coup d'etat is formulated, brought about, and the aftermath. What is astounding about this interview is that Ayers apparently had no qualms about eliminating huge numbers of American citizens who might be die-hard capitalists, who are diametrically opposed to his new form of government. When asked directly by Grathwohl about what would need to be done with these "counter revolutionaries" he replied that they would need to be eliminated. When asked how many people he thought that might be, Ayers responds…perhaps 25 million. So, to be clear, we are talking about a post-capitalist system whose architect casually mentions the elimination (killing) of tens of millions of Americans.

Bill Ayers true beliefs have gone deeper underground and have become more insidious and deceptive since that time. But the fact remains that he is the person interviewed by an FBI informant, Grathwohl, who shares the following in an on-camera interview.

---

12 Weather Underground and the reeducating the new order people, from (1982) documentary *"No Place to Hide: The Strategy and Tactics of Terrorism"* excerpted at https://www.youtube.com/watch?v=XBtANp4IKVk

I asked, "Well, what is going to happen to those people we can't reeducate, that are diehard capitalist?" And the reply was that they'd have to be eliminated.

And when I pursued this further, they estimated they would have to eliminate 25 million people in these reeducation centers.

And when I say "eliminate," I mean "kill."

Twenty-five million people.

I want you to imagine sitting in a room with 25 people, most of which have graduate degrees, from Columbia and other well-known educational centers, and hear them figuring out the logistics of the elimination of 25 million people; and they are dead serious.[13]

After this documentary aired on HBO in 1982, the cat was let completely out of the bag, so to speak. But Ayers knew years before it aired that he needed to keep a low profile. And it would be several years before he would surface again publicly. In this period he apparently matured and grew even more industrious with regard to how to take down Imperialist America.

A Bloodless Revolution was the avenue Ayers and his associates would need to travel in today's society because he finally determined that destroying property and killing people was not going to win over the hearts and minds of new recruits. It's actually quite humorous that Ayers came to that conclusion after such a long time, when one considers his academic prowess. But as intellectually accomplished as Ayers was, it must have been the vitriol and hatred with which he perceived American exceptionalism that blinded him for a time to a bloodless path.

---

13 Ibid.

Ayers's disdain for the American system, the ultra-rich and the political elite, along with being a self-proclaimed socialist, is what would now fuel his methods and support the means by which he would make his play for revolution within systems, rather than by attacking them. After a dozen years to mature and grow academically, Ayers began to see that a Bloody Revolution was not practical, and he began to take certain measures to change his tack. He saw that America cannot be transformed by bullet, but by ballot. The process will be long and arduous. But it can be done, and he sees where the starting point is: **our schools—K thru 12.**

THE NEW BATTLEGROUND: OUR ELEMENTARY SCHOOLS

This will be the new battleground for Ayers and his comrades Bloodless Revolution. At this point, Ayers already had several people who had set the stage and begun the assault, which I discuss in the next chapter. But little had been accomplished by the late 1980s because of two key elements: the right rhetorical spokesmen of color had yet to emerge, and the modern Mainstream Media –including Ted Turner's CNN, had not yet fully emerged to be exploited by the cause.

Perhaps a major reason that Ayers is not only unrepentant, but does not publicly admit to a major shift in his vocation between 1974 and today, is that he never made a meaningful change in his true vision; only a change in his approach. Put simply, destroying government property and issuing propaganda in the 1970s is nothing compared to successfully commandeering the minds of America's school children. And the proof is now surrounding us.

Now I mustn't let one individual go un-accounted for in this academic precursor to fundamental social change. This person's teachings have for several years now, poured a racist poison into the ears and minds of tens of thousands of young people across America.

Michael Eric Dyson is a professor of Sociology at Georgetown University. It is clear that his ideal, that racism in America is out of control, that the white-privileged hierarchy here in this country has a stranglehold on politics, and that these institutions and corporations' power must be mitigated. To hear his statements, it is as if Martin Luther King had not accomplished a single thing. And Dyson preaches this on a daily basis: that America is institutionally racist. He never mentions Colin Powell, or Oprah, or Condoleezza Rice or Supreme Court Justice Clarence Thomas. He clings to Tupac, Jay-Z and Marvin Gay. Oh, and President Barack Obama.

Dyson has written more than a dozen books that highlight the black experience and how oppressive American institutions are and how the racial divide is due to the white-privileged hierarchy in America. He is convinced that white privilege exists in America to such a degree that all people of color must fight the white controlled establishment and usher in a newer, less bigoted system. One with no hatred for people of color.

Here is the thing about Dyson that intrigues me. He is riding this wave of socialist anti-Americanism that we are seeing be played out every day on the liberal-biased mainstream media. This Anti-American movement that is pointed at our conservative values is a central part of the Liberal/ Marxist Machine's narrative. The narrative that is taking up so much of the Liberal playbook is that the white privileged hierarchy in America, and the very beginnings of America, including the entire system we have here, is "Oppressive" for people of color. It is racist by nature, and innately de-structive to a fair and just society. To Dyson, this mindset is inherent in this country and it's a stain that must be removed. When one hears him relate this ideal of his, he is the modern-day carnival barker, mimicking Malcom X before Malcolm came to his senses. And the fact that Malcolm did come to his senses is what compelled his associates, his very own brothers in the arena, to murder him.

Dyson has a job. It is to preach to America—all adult white Americans, as well to impressionable very young white Americans—that they must un-derstand this historical oppression dominates the modern day landscape. They must learn to give up their inborn bigotry and hatred of people of color and throw away the shackles of preconceived notions of color and ignorance. Dyson's book, *Sermon to White America*, explains in detail how the poor disenfranchised black Americans are victims of American society as a whole.[14]

Not to be redundant, but to me, it truly is as if Martin Luther King did not accomplish a single thing. It's as if the Civil Rights movement of the fifties and sixties had zero effect on the American psyche. Dyson continues his Marxist dialectic lectures all around the country on college and university campuses. He has professed himself to be the holder of the MLK banner, but he proves himself to be a pretender to the throne. It is now his job to show everyone how racist they are; at least all white folk. He has called Jordan Peterson, who is loved by millions as a public speaker and logician, "An Angry Hate-Filled White Man."[15]

So here is my take on how and why Dyson continues to press race. The longer Dyson brings race and white privilege into the discussion, the longer it will take for people to move beyond our colonial history, beyond the Civil War and reconstruction, and the longer he can continue to preach and earn a living. Racism is not a white only paradigm. Racism exists when one group believes they are inherently superior to another. It has existed in every culture to some extent since the beginning of time. However, I do not accept that white privilege dominates the landscape here in America as Dyson would have everyone believe. Stories and perceptions are exaggerated, and Dyson is masterful in reliance upon anecdote and emotion more than reasoned analysis of evidence. And here is where the media play a determinant role, where the mainstream is "played" by ever-increasing socialist propaganda. The phrase "if it bleeds, it leads" has been used to describe how relatively easy it is for media advocates to make the news. So while few would suggest Jordan Peterson is a household name, the left-leaning media have ensured that Professor Dyson is. After all, when would

---

14 Dyson, EM. **Tears We Cannot Stop: A Sermon to White America** (2017) St. Martin's Press. ISBN: 9781250135995

15 The Munk Debates- Political Correctness; May 18, 2018; Toronto, Ontario, CA. https://www. youtube.com/watch?v=MNjYSns0op0

CNN, NBC or even CSPAN let facts and reason get in the way of heartfelt and tearful coverage of race-based discrimination?

Here is a quote from a very intelligent fellow from way back in the earlier years of this country, circa 1889:

> "There is a class of colored people who make a business of keeping the troubles, and the wrongs and the hardships of the negro race before the public. Some folks do not want the negro to lose his grievances because they do not want to lose their jobs. There is a class of problem solvers who do not want the patient to get well."
>
> - Booker T. Washington

I offer up the comment by a conservative activist that, when push comes to shove, liberals are going to lose—and lose big—in the "Victimhood Game." At the Oxford Union debate of May 12, 2015, David Webb, an African American conservative argued that the United States is not institutionally racist. He explains that to be so would require at least two conditions, creating the environment necessary. These are first, a Social Contract, such as existed in the antebellum South, and Codified Law, to sustain the environment. Because these are not in fact in place, Webb argues not only that the United States cannot be institutionally racist today, but that people like the Reverend Al Sharpton lack the moral courage to admit that they are perpetuating a false narrative.

This conflict we see today is best seen for what it is: planned "Class/Culture/Political Warfare." And Mr. Webb asks us in his address to be extremely cautious when we hear the term "systemic or institutional racism." This is the Marxists influence, the Socialist shadow pointing the finger of blame at all white folks and their inherently racist system that they commissioned to keep blacks down…But which, incredibly, has improved the quality of life for virtually every human on the planet.

What we see today from Professor Dyson and BLM movement is precisely the Marxist dialectic. This is the catalyst for conflict between the classes and the cultures that Marx predicted would be the seeds for the destruction of Western Capitalism.

Karl Marx saw the only solution as revolution and total equality among people. Vladimir Lenin called out to them, the proletariat: "Workers of the world must unite, and demand their rights." The only real solution was a world without classes. None better, none worse. All people in one big class. This was the utopia Karl Marx envisioned, with everyone working for a common state, and the state would provide. And there would be no need for strife.

But poor Karl couldn't see past his ideals. He knew hope would be gone. He knew that every single person would never be able to live out a dream. And he omitted that in his manifesto. The perceived inequities and actual examples of brutality, pushed day after day about poor and disenfranchised Blacks in America was Uncle Sam's "knee on their necks." And this is the only news that sells. And these are the stories shown to the masses. Day by day, hour after hour, and re-posted on social media minute by minute, by the Liberal/Marxist Machine, then amplified by the mainstream media. Often exaggerated, many times out-of-context, but nonetheless consistent with the socialist narrative, this is what children see. And the effects are enormous.

No references or documentaries on how mankind is making leaps and bounds into space exploration, or medicine, or simply the phenomenal quality of life enjoyed by most Americans.

Nothing but bad news on America and Americans. Because that is what sells.

This Marxist dialectic is what spawned Black Lives Matter. And the extremely sad part is that this disparity that people have lived with for centuries, these inequities that come with being free, are now fair game for the Machine and fuel for anarchy. Fuel for destruction. And these differences have somehow gotten blown so far out of proportion that there is no going back.

Racism appears in every corner of the globe, but it is not inborn. It is learned. It is "conditioned." More importantly racism is a secondary emotion. Hate and ignorance is what drives race-based discrimination. And hate is driven by fear and fueled by ignorance.

People like Michael Eric Dyson continually perpetuate the narrative that he, along with those who support his views, can somehow eliminate racism from existence by putting it front-and-center in the political/social discourse. As if racism can be extinguished by educating the masses and changing their mindset. That people of color are exempt and cannot possibly pose a threat. That's the Marxist game in its purest form.

The threat? Do white folks pose a threat? Do black folks? Michael Eric Dyson views white folks as an existential threat to the very existence of people of color, mostly black people. Well, ladies and gentlemen, let me point out one extremely poignant observation Mr. Dyson has been recorded preaching to white Americans; that black folks cannot be racist. Read his words for yourself. Recorded from a Black Entertainment Television event where he was to speak. This short rant speaks volumes. And let me point out that Michael Eric Dyson claims to be from the projects of Detroit. He has street credibility. I beg to differ. Dyson came from outside the City of Detroit. . . the suburbs of Bloomfield Hills. Have a peek at reality folks. . . and you decide whether to eat what you're being fed.

From a BET event where Dyson recorded a one minute and fifty second rant on how "Black people cannot be racist."[16]

> "For those of you who have heard similar viewpoints espoused by similar people. . . let me tell you this: that kind of lethal ignorance. . . that kind of viewpoint that, disparages black people, number one, that condescends and talks down to us, number two, that draws specious, spurious parallels between white racism and black racism... Racism

16 Backstage at Don't Sleep! Black Entertainment Television (2015) https://www.youtube.com/watch?v=bZ0QfLkjujY

presupposes the ability to control a significant segment of the population economically, politically, and socially by imposing law, covenant and restriction on their lives."

Now here is one of my favorites. His very next line in the rant: "Black people ain't had no capacity to do that." Meaning that blacks in America have no power in America yet, institutionally speaking. Wow. What a statement. Dyson just told Supreme Court Justice Clarence Thomas that he is incapable of wielding power. And perhaps by this logic the rest of the academic giants in America who are black are too ignorant to possess any real power either.

His next line in this rant is priceless. "Can black people be bigoted. . . Yes! Prejudiced. . . Yes! Racist. . . No!" And my all-time favorite: "the un-intelligence of the formulation is problematic when any black person says that." Makes me laugh every time I read that line.

But getting back to "The Threat." I, for one, never saw a person of color as a threat. But Michael Eric Dyson see's white power structure in America as the predominant entity that keeps black folks down. And you know what; every adult in the audience can see the vitriol with which he looks down at white folks. He demonizes whiteness as if it were some demographic that innately breeds ignorance, bigotry, and hatred for people of color.

Today, in halls and campuses around America, Dyson continues preaching that racism in America is flourishing now more than ever. And this only exacerbates the problem that actually has existed since time began. Bigotry and racism will never be extinguished. It is part of the human condition and adults can see this. But only as individuals can we decide to put it aside.

It is disgusting. It's the Liberal/Marxist Machine's narrative and it is dangerous. But the best part of the entire Dyson sermon we must endure is that we can hear him coming. Thoughtful people in the room know where he stands, and we can walk the other way. Unfortunately, some children, the very young ones, cannot just walk away. They get indoctrinated with the Dyson Doctrine in school. Even especially the college-aged young adults. It is poison by nature, and destructive in form

Now, in complete contrast, let me bring in the perspectives of an authority on these disparities and inequities we seem to be hearing so much about, Dr. Thomas Sowell.

Dr. Sowell was born in North Carolina but grew up in Harlem. After serving in the Marines, he received a BA from Harvard graduating magna cum laude in 1958. A Masters from Columbia and then a PhD in Economics from the University of Chicago. Importantly, Dr. Sowell has written more than thirty books, several of which have been reprinted in revised editions . . . and they are on topics where Sowell is considered to be an authority by academics around the world.

What intrigues me about Dr. Sowell is his complete and total understanding of the topics he writes about and especially when interviewed and asked specific questions. He is able to answer in a short sentence or two. Not a stretched-out version with academese to sound intelligent. He already knows he is intelligent. And that is his authenticity. That is his understandability.

Let me take you on a ride with Dr. Sowell through these disparities by which we are so dominated; or at least the mainstream media and radical left wing organization seem to believe we are. Let us begin with one quote from the good doctor, and this is not news. It's reality.

> "Although most black owners of slaves in the US were only nominal owners of members of their own families, there were thousands of other blacks in the Antebellum South who were commercial slave owners, just like their white counterparts. An estimated 1/3 of the "Freepersons of Color" in New Orleans were slave owners and thousands of these black slave owners volunteered to fight for the Confederacy in the Civil War."[17]

---

17 Sowell, Thomas. *Black rednecks and white liberals.* 2005, © Encounter books, San Francisco

This information is never talked about and the Liberal/Marxist Machine wants it to be silenced by the mainstream media. Now, have a good look at true intellectual prowess: a paper by Dr. Sowell on these inequalities we are so dominated by, but as a people, and as a nation, we have lived with for centuries.

H. G. Goerner

RACE, CULTURE, AND EQALITY[1]
By Thomas Sowell

During the 15 years that I spent researching and writing my recently completed trilogy on racial and cultural issues.[2] I was struck again and again with how common huge disparities in income and wealth have been for centuries, in countries around the world-- and yet how each country regards its own particular disparities as unusual, if not unique. Some of these disparities have been among racial or ethnic groups, some among nations, and some among regions, continents, or whole civilizations.

In the nineteenth century, real per capita income in the Balkans was about one-third that in Britain. That dwarfs intergroup disparities that many in the United States today regard as not merely strange but sinister. Singapore has a median per capita income that is literally hundreds of times greater than that in Burma.

During the rioting in Indonesia last year, much of it directed against the ethnic Chinese in that country, some commentators found it strange that the Chinese minority, which is just 5 percent of the Indonesian population, owned an estimated four-fifths of the capital in the country. But it is not strange. Such disparities have long been common in other countries in Southeast Asia, where Chinese immigrants typically entered poor and then prospered, creating whole industries in the process. People from India did the same in much of East Africa and in Fiji.

Occupations have been similarly unequal

In the early 1920s, Jews were just 6 percent of the population of Hungary and 11 percent of the population of Poland, but they were more than half of all the physicians in both countries, as well as being vastly over-represented in commerce and other fields.[3] In the early twentieth century, all of the firms in all of the industries producing the following products in Brazil's state of Rio Grande do Sul were owned by people of German ancestry: trunks, stoves, paper, hats, neckties, leather, soap, glass, watches, beer, confections and carriages.[4] In the middle of the nineteenth century, just three countries produced most of the manufactured goods in the world-- Britain, Germany, and the United States. By the late twentieth century, it was estimated that 17 percent of the people in the world produce four-fifths of the total output on the planet.

Such examples could be multiplied longer than you would have the patience to listen.[5]

Why are there such disparities? In some cases, we can trace the reasons, but in other cases we cannot. A more fundamental question, however, is: Why should anyone have ever expected equality in the first place?

Let us assume, for the sake of argument, that not only every racial or ethnic group, but even every single individual in the entire world, has identical genetic potential. If it is possible to be even more extreme, let us assume that we all behave like saints toward one another

Would that produce equality of results?

Of course not. Real income consists of output and output depends on inputs. These inputs are almost never equal-- or even close to being equal. [end]

Here is the beauty of input versus output. The more you put into it, the more you will get out of it. Not everyone is going to put in the same amount, but it is a reality that the more you put in, the more you'll get out. Here in America, you are allowed to put in as much as you want. And everyone knows with their eyes wide open, going in how much input is needed. The beauty is; it is up to the individual to decide. This is the basis of Meritocracy. The more you are able to contribute to society, the more you benefit AND the society as a whole benefits.

3

The Method and the Marxist/
Ayers Connection

THE MARXIST DIALECTIC

This is where Ayers got his inspiration and early education for a new and promising America that he would dangle out in front of impressionable, idealistic young students of a Utopian Nation. A nation and society free of all oppression, racism, and white supremacy. He saw socialism and communism as a vehicle to begin his assault on American values, culture, and ideals, and he would use the writings from a communist manifesto from the 1800s. He learned these backwards societies could be economically viable in America. . . IF, he could cause enough dissent to provoke a kind of revolution.

A brief history lesson showed that it was around 1848 that Karl Marx published his Communist Manifesto. From there Russian society would take a turn for what the world would see as the USSR seventy-four years later. The USSR's value however, lay in its enormous mass of land, resources and human population, and those economic values were sustained for several years until its demise in December 1991.

Ayers dove deep into these lessons.

The eventual formation of the U.S.S.R. would require Vladimir Ilyich Ulyanov [Lenin] and Lev Davidovich Bronshtein [Trotsky] to convince the workers (i.e., the proletariat) that the bourgeoisie and political leaders—especially the rich—were evil, and a revolution was needed to bring about change. Lenin ended up being dictator upon the birth of the Union of Soviet Socialist Republic on Dec. 30, 1922, and ultimately Stalin moved in right after his death in 1924. It would be Stalin that would show the world what atrocities come with a totalitarian form government.[18]

All of us that paid attention in school know about the millions that Lenin and Stalin murdered and starved. But Ayers learned that a bloody revolution would not be successful in America. Eventually, it would take a bloodless revolution, where the proletariat [the people] with Cuba and China's help, would force the new government in place, and Ayers would proclaim himself leader. But it was a shallow thought process. Neither clear nor demonstrative. Only youth, hubris, and anarchy. Here is the absurdity of Ayers's bloodless revolution. Like Lenin and the Bolsheviks bloodless revolution some blood would have to be spilled. The Bolsheviks and Lenin would convince the proletariat workers to rise up. As Lenin put it, "Workers of the world. . . unite" and claim what is yours. Then you assassinate the Tsar of Russia and his entire family.

Let's look briefly at the significant events that led to the execution of the Czar Nicholas Alexandrovich Romanov II. He is better known as Saint Nicholas the Passion-Bearer. He was the last Russian ruler of the dynasty that reigned for over 300 years.

Nicholas II ruled Russia for 23 years, but he was ill-prepared and even reluctant to be Czar of Russia. His attempts to rule competently were fruitless and proved to be his undoing. He was not up to the task and, toward the end, he sought to abdicate. He asked Britain and France to take him in. Both declined, and he was stuck. The Bolsheviks finally forced him out of the Catherine Palace and took control of Russia. Nicholas, his wife, and children were held captive for months in the basement of an old building. Awaiting their fate. Finally, on the evening of July 17, 1918, instead of allowing Nicholas and his family to just leave Russia forever, a carefully planned execution of the Czar and his entire family was carried out by the

---

18 Naimark, N. *Stalin's Genocides*. 2011. © Princeton University Press.

Bolsheviks. The Czar, his wife and five children were shot repeatedly and bayoneted, and the bodies incinerated.

Let this brief history lesson show how even bloodless revolutions are never bloodless. People across the country—any country that have revolutionaries stalking the roads and by-ways to stir their hatred for the government—will never do it peacefully. Blood will be shed, and it will not be theirs. . . it will be ours. Patriotic Americans that love this country will be the ones who lose and bleed. The Liberal/Marxist Machine will stop at nothing to secure the "Transformation," violate all rules and shed our blood for their power.

Today we are witnessing the beginnings of the push by the Machine to make that happen. The actual process of pushing a country to the brink of revolution would have to begin with decades of dissent, poverty, and oppression. In 1850 Russia there was plenty of that. But here in America, these conditions did not exist.

For Ayer's revolution, he would have to convince the American proletariat that they have been "kept down" on purpose. Even with a strong economy and the quality of life for the even the poorest in America at its highest in a century, Ayers would persuade the oppressed that the they are part of the "systematic oppression" which is being led by the political and corporate "elites" here in America. Especially older white male corporate CEO's, congressmen, and senators.

Ayers' perception of a White supremacy in America, and the hierarchy that ran the country was going to be his mantra. In his book "Race Course Against White Supremacy", Ayers relates exactly how twisted he is with regard to his perception of "Hierarchy." Ayers saw America through this lens of provocative anti-social and pathological misconceptions. America is and has always been the vanguard of white supremacy and total disregard for the oppressed and poor. It is as if Ayers understood only one thing. . . "America was built on the backs of the poor, disenfranchised and blacks." The entire colonial upstarts were "old white men". And ever since, people of color and the poor, he asserts, have been kept down for a reason. What that reason is, however, he never reveals. He would put in motion an aggressive campaign that would call out the white male hierarchy. The systematic racism. The oppressive nuances toward the immigrant and the newcomer to America, that had existed from the very outset, as well as the domestic American imperialist doctrine that persisted throughout the nation and around the world.

Ayers was, and is, a Communist/Anarchist by admission. He wanted to see anarchy and revolution. He knew his path, and he immersed himself in it. But as a newcomer in the Socialism game, he had his work cut out for him, and that much he understood. He would discover later on that there was a little-known resource that he could plunder, and he would direct his aim on that resource in the early 1980's, a point we will cover after we review the socialist ideal he would incorporate into his mantra.

It now seems funny because Ayers overlooked a little-known economic theory call Ricardian Socialism. This theory puts a positive light on the socialist concept; and the economics of it are sound. However, its success depended on cooperation and contributions from everyone. David Ricardo theorized that a socialist nation would work. . . if (1) the economy expanded, and (2) everyone contributed.

The results would be that everyone would share equally in the proceeds and benefits. If you could not contribute equally, you would receive appropriate benefits aligned with your contributions. It was Ricardo's concept of . . . "to each according to his contribution" that showed promise.[19]

This theory would and could work, but during that time the population was still relatively small and population would have a huge effect on the workings of a socialist economy. Socialism can only work when the population of a region or country is stable or at least constant. When a population of that region grows rapidly, costs increase drastically. A relatively small country with a stable population and strong tax system would be able to thrive. A large country like the United States would find population growth and social services a real threat to its economic survival.

19 Noel W. Thompson. *Ricardian socialists/Smithian socialists: what's in a name.* (2010) Publisher: Cambridge University Press

However, to Karl Marx, this is where things start to go south, "From each according to his contribution or his ability to each according to his needs." He wants everyone in the state to be taken care of, whether you contribute or not. But Lenin and Stalin put their own twist on it: If you are unable to contribute, you would be a liability.

This is where Karl's theory breaks down. Ultimately it was the individual that would benefit and suffer at the same time. And suffer they did. If you dissented, declined or were unable to contribute you would be a liability, and you would be dealt this accordingly. Liabilities were considered a threat to the State.

The STATE was ALL. . . and the individual was only a resource.

There would be no private ownership and all benefits from production would be equally dispersed. In this system the masses got fed, housed, and clothed and there was only "working class" and the political hierarchy. That was the state system. Everything dispersed equally and no need to complain. OR DREAM. All hope of an individual dreams was gone. But the state survived and continued on.

And I discovered something else during my research: President Obama and his influence.

Marx's idea for a nation was right in line with Obama's Affordable Care Act, as well as many of the other nationalist moves. A single payer system that was basically socialized medicine. This was just the beginning for Obama and the nationalization of most all the programs that belonged solely to the States.

And please, do not disregard President Obama's Affordable Care Act. This and many other Obama programs dramatically shifted the federal governments influence over everything. The architect of Obama's Socialized Health Care was Jonathan Gruber. An MIT whiz kid that would spill the beans in a three-minute explanation of just how Obama perpetrated this on America. Gruber explains, "The lack of transparency is a huge political advantage." And my personal favorite. . . "If the American people knew it was a single payer system, the bill never would have passed".[20]

In addition to hearing Gruber talk about how the Affordable Care Act was written in such a tortured way at this time, the ACA was not the only "change" Americans saw. There was Common Core State Standards, as well as a few other well-timed additions.

OBAMA-AYERS CONNECTION

Obama broke a dozen rules and shoved Common Core and his ACA down America's throat which added to the dissent and he knew it. It was nothing more than socialized medicine that the middle and upper class would pay for and the poor would benefit from. It was a "top-down, bottom-up" leveling affect that the liberal political leaders just pushed through without any discussion. Even Supreme Court Justice Roberts altered the ACA language from "penalty" to "tax." The Supreme Court now had become legislators.

And Common Core was convened in private. The best explanation for "seeing" the complexity of Obama's manipulation the system and how he literally dangled TARP money in front of governors that desperately needed funds because their states were insolvent, can been seen in the documentary "Common Core: Building the Machine." In this 45-minute video, a diagram of the complexities and consequences of a new education system is brought to the forefront. There is an additional must-see second video that accompanies the first, "Parents Interviews" on the subject. In this second video, the reality of just how destructive common Core is to individual kids is revealed with devastating effect.[21]

20 Thiessen, M. Washington Post (November 17, 2014), *Thanks to Jonathan Gruber for revealing Obamacare deception.*
https://www.washingtonpost.com/opinions/marc-thiessen-thanks-to-jonathan-gruber-for-revealing-obamacare-deception/2014/11/17/356514b2-6e72-11e4-893f-86bd390a3340_story.html

21 Building the Machine, Ian Anthony Reid, An investigative documentary into the Common Core State Standards Initiative, produced by Home School Legal Defense Association, 2014. Vimeo: https://vimeo.com/97016931

The parent interviews on <u>Building the Machine</u> bring home how radical Common Core was to the learning curve for adolescents. Interviews from several counselors and psychologists show an increase in children not being able to cope with the new standards. You will hear dozens of arguments that push the narrative CCSS are State-run, and are a State program, and a state curriculum. Nothing could be further from the truth. Obama initiated and essentially nationalized our education systems. Have a peek at Neal McCluskey's insistence on getting the facts right in this CATO Institute article, exposing the facts about CCSS.

We've been fighting over the Common Core national curriculum standards for years now, and at this point the people who "fact check" ought to know the facts. Also, at this point, I should be doing many other things than laying out basic truths about the Core. Yet here I am, about to fact-check fact-checking by The Seventy Four, an education news and analysis site set up by former television journalist Campbell Brown. Thankfully, I am not alone in having to repeat this Sisyphean chore; AEI's Rick Hess did the same thing addressing Washington Post fact-checkers yesterday.

Because I have done this **so many times before** – what follows are relatively quick, clarifications beneath the "facts" the "fact check" missed.

In a text box FACT: It was the states — more specifically the Council of Chief State School Officers and National Governors Association — that developed the standards. During the Obama administration, the Education Department has played no specific role in the implementation of those standards, and the classroom curriculum used to meet the broad goals set out in Common Core is created by districts and states, as it always has been. Further, states have made tweaks to the Common Core standards since their initial adoption and, in some cases, have decided to drop the standards entirely.

- The Council of Chief State School Officers (CCSSO) and National Governors Association

(NGA) are *not* states. They are, essentially, professional associations of governors and state superintendents. And they are definitely not legislatures, which much more than governors represent "the people" of their states. So no, it was not "states" that developed the standards.

- The CCSSO and NGA explicitly called for federal influence to move states onto common, internationally benchmarked standards – what the Core is supposed to be – writing in the 2008 report *Benchmarking for Success* that the role of the federal government is to offer "incentives" to get states to use common standards, including offering funding and regulatory relief. See **page 7 of the report**, and note that the same information was once on the Common Core website but has since been removed.

- The Common Core was dropped into a federally dictated system under the No Child Left Behind Act that required accountability based on state standards and tests, so Washington did have a role in overseeing "implementation" of the standards. And since what is tested for accountability purposes is what is supposed to get taught, it is very deceptive to say, simply, curriculum "is created by districts and states." The curricula that states create are supposed to be heavily influenced by Core, and especially the math section pushes specific content. Indeed, the Core calls specifically for **instructional "shifts."** Oh, and the federal government selected and funded two consortia of states to create national tests – the Partnership for the Assessment of Readiness for College and Career (PARCC) and the Smarter-Balanced Assessment Consortium (SBAC) – which the Department of Education, to at least some extent, **oversaw.**

FACT: States competing for Race to the Top funds in 2009 got more points on their application for the adoption of "internationally benchmarked standards and assessments that prepare students for success in college and the workplace." Adopting those standards won a state 40 points out of 500 possible, according to the National Conference of State Legislatures.

Congress has not funded Race to the Top grants in the annual appropriations process for several years, and several states – notably Oklahoma and Indiana – have dropped the Common Core.

- The $4. 35 billion Race to the Top was the primary lever to coerce states into Core adoption, and it did far more than give 40 out of 500 points for adopting any ol' "internationally benchmarked standards and assessments." It came as close to saying Common Core as possible without actually saying Common Core, which, by the way, **reporting by the** *Washington Post***'s Lyndsey Layton** suggested the Obama administration wanted to do, but was asked not to because the optics would be bad. So instead the regulations said that to get maximum points states would have to adopt standards common to a "majority" of states – a definition *only* *met by the Core* – and went to pains to make sure the adoption timelines suited the Core....

- It is true that the Race to the Top pushing Core implementation only happened once – though in multiple phases – but the Obama administration later cemented it by only giving **two choices of standards** to get waivers out of the most dreaded parts of the No Child Left behind Act: either have standards common to a "significant number of states," or a public university system certify a state's own standards as "college- and career-ready." And all of this happened after states had promised to use the Core in Race to the Top; it would have been tough for state officials to suddenly say they would not use the Core because, well, they only promised to do so for the federal money.

FACT: Federal law already prohibits the government from forcing states to adopt Common Core.

The Every Student Succeeds Act, which Obama signed into law in December, **includes 13 references to the Common Core – all limitations on federal power to meddle in curriculum** [*emphasis added*].

Specifically from the law: "No officer or employee of the federal government shall, through grants, contracts, or other cooperative agreements, mandate, direct, or control a state, local education agency, or school's specific instructional content, academic standards and assessments, curricula, or other program of instruction...including any requirement, direction, or mandate to adopt the Common Core State Standards."

To the contrary, ESSA specifically protects states' rights to "enter into a voluntary partnership with another state to develop and implement" challenging academic standards.

- This "fact" was invoked to counter promises by Republican presidential candidates to end Common Core if elected. And it is correct that the ESSA singles out the Core as something that cannot be specifically coerced. But, of course, *that has already essentially happened*, and it is worth noting that federal law has had paper against federal influence over curriculum for decades. Precious good they did, not that forcing states to dump the Core would be any more constitutional than the original coercion.

FACT: The federal government already has a limited role in K-12 education. Particularly in the wake of the passage of the Every Student Succeeds Act, the primary federal roles are providing supplemental funds for the education of children in poverty (the Title I program), setting standards for the education of children with disabilities and helping fund those services (the Individuals with Disabilities Education Act), and ensuring children don't go hungry (the school lunch program, which is run through the Agriculture Department.)

The monetary role is small, too. According to federal data, between 1980 and 2011, between 7 and 13 percent of total annual education funding came from federal sources.

And only about half of that funding in 2011 came from the Education Department. Another quarter of that funding came from the Department of Agriculture for the school lunch program. The Defense Department (junior reserve officers' training program and their own school system for students of military members), Health and Human Services (Head Start pre-school) and about a half-dozen other departments for smaller programs made up the rest.

- The federal government has taken on a largely *un-limited* role in education – everything from funding to coercing curriculum standards – which is why we saw anger on both the left and right spur passage of the ESSA. But it is not clear that the ESSA reduces the federal role to simply providing supplemental funds, standards for children with disabilities, and stopping hunger. The new law requires that states send standard, testing, and accountability plans to Washington for approval; requires uniform statewide testing; and demands interventions in the worst performing schools, among other things. And this is before the regulations – which some groups are **pushing to be very prescriptive** – have been written.

- Oh, the school lunch program? It is also about **pushing what Washington deems** to be proper nutrition and balanced diets on schools, not just "ensuring children don't go hungry."

- It is true that the monetary role as a percentage of total spending is kind of small, but roughly ten percent of funding isn't nothing, and federal funding was in much demand during the nadir of the Great Recession, when Race to the Top was in effect. And it is very hard to be a politician in any state and say, "I'm going to turn down this $100 million, or that $1 billion, because it's not that big a percentage of our funding." This is something of which federal politicians are well aware, and spending **roughly $80 billion on K-12** is not chump change, even by federal standards.

FACT: Abolishing the federal Education Department would also wipe out the Office of Innovation and Improvement, which oversees the very initiatives Cruz wants to promote: federal efforts to spur more charter schools and magnet schools; the DC Opportunity Scholarship Program, the only federal school voucher program; and the Office of Non-Public Education.

- Ironically, after downplaying federal influence in education, The Seventy Four tweaks Presidential candidate Ted Cruz for saying he wants to get rid of the U. S. Department of Education and expand school choice. So while suggesting overall federal spending is kind of puny at 7 to 13 percent of the total, apparently Department of Education spending on charter school grants is too big to kill. But it is only $333 million dollars, or about $147 per charter student. That is a princely 1 percent of what the U. S. spends, on average, per K-12 student. Meanwhile, the DC voucher program is constantly under threat of destruction. And none of these justify keeping the Department which does way, WAY more than these few things.

So there it is, as fast as I could get it out. No doubt I missed some things. But hopefully this is enough for the fact checkers to get things closer to accurate next time. And now, on to other things...[22]

In this piece, McKluskey points out that this was a federally mandated program, and he describes the very lack of transparency with which Common Core was instituted. Let me point out one additional item of import. Whenever a federal meeting on matters of such public interest are convened, a public noticing is required. According to the federal sunshine act, "every portion of every meeting of an agency shall be open to public observation."[23] This mandate applies to the meetings and discussions by heads of any federal government agency. This is apparently did not happen, and therefore constitutes a violation. Let us now get even more specific and return to the time leading up to his time in public office. Several years before Obama became a Senator, (and Common Core became a reality), then professor Obama was lecturing and teaching at the Chicago University Law School. This is when he began working closely with Bill Ayers as both were on the Chicago Annenberg Challenge Board of Directors (CAC).

What is the Chicago Annenberg Challenge? The CAC was the brain-child for Ayers to fund his school reformation. In 1995 President Clinton and publishing magnate Warren Annenberg announced a 500-million-dollar endowment program called the Annenberg Challenge, that was to be matched by private and government funds to improve the education system here in America.

You will hear dozens of arguments that push the narrative that CCSS (Common Core State Standards) are state-run educational programs.

22 Neal McCluskey, **Getting the Common Core (and Federal) Facts Right.** (2016) https://www.cato.org/blog/getting-common-core-federal-facts-right

23 U.S. General Services Administration- GSA. *Government in the Sunshine Act.* https://www.gsa.gov/policy-regulations/policy/federal-advisory-committee-management/statutes-and-related-legislation

Common Core "State" Standards are not "State run standards at all – Under President Obama, the federal government initiated CCSS and "nationalized" America's education program.

Ayers went to work immediately to set up a team to apply for the grant and believe it or not. Ayers' proposal for the regional 50 million was a shoe-in. He worked closely with the regional and national directors of the Annenberg Foundation and discussions were recorded and the money was already on its way [so to speak] and spent. All he needed to do was apply. And sign the document. Illinois [at the time] had failing school children across the state and Chicago inner city children had Ayers to thank for the incoming dollars to be passed around in his Street Schools and ACORN.

Ladies and gentlemen, let me bring in the voice of an authority on the subject of education and let you judge for yourselves. This gentleman that is no longer with us but who has my deepest respect and admiration for his insights and understanding of the real reasons children today are failing in the inner city schools. His name is Andrew J. Coulson. He was a Senior Fellow at the CATO Institute and had written dozens and dozens of articles for numerous academic periodicals. In his National Review article from 2008, Coulson outlines how Ayers and Obama pushed through the 1995 CAC without any real foundation for replication of an academic system that was working, yet Ayers could manipulate for his "Social Justice" education theory. The CAC was a catalyst in 1995 for bigger and better things to come. But at the time, CAC was up and rolling Ayers could implement an education curriculum that would begin to take shape as Common Core that eventually Obama could nationalize across America.[24]

---

24 Andrew J. Coulson *Markets vs. Monopolies in Education: A Global Review of the Evidence.* October 27, 2008. Cato Institute, Center for Educational Freedom. https://www.cato.org/publications/commentary/wreck-annenberg

October 27, 2008

THE WRECK OF THE ANNENBERG

By Andrew J. Coulson

This article appeared in the *National Review Online* on October 27, 2008.

THANKS TO BILL AYERS, A GREAT MANY PEOPLE NOW KNOW THAT Barack Obama chaired the board of the Chicago Annenberg Challenge from 1995 to 1999. Ayers, erstwhile member of the 60s' terrorist group, the Weather Underground, was the driving force in bringing Annenberg's millions of education reform dollars to Chicago, and he worked with Obama once the project was up and running.

It was inevitable that political hay would be made from this link, but in the process a more fundamental insight has been overlooked: The Chicago Annenberg Challenge was a total failure. And to this day, Senator Obama remains committed to its failed approach.

But instead of being in a position to waste tens of millions of private dollars, as he was then, Obama is now asking voters for the power to waste hundreds of billions of taxpayer dollars. Before granting him that power, Americans should understand what went wrong.

The Chicago Annenberg Challenge was part of a nationwide effort launched by *TV Guide* mogul Walter H. Annenberg on a blustery December day in 1993. In a White House ceremony hosted by President Clinton, Annenberg pledged half a billion dollars to create model public schools and districts. He and the scholars he appointed to lead the project hoped their models of excellence would be replicated all over the country, transforming American education. Thanks to matching donations, the Challenge ultimately raised more than a billion dollars.

It failed not just in Chicago, but around the country. The first problem was that many of the "model" schools and districts lacked results worthy of replication. The final report of the Chicago Annenberg Challenge, for instance, noted that, overall, students in its model schools had learned no more than students in regular public schools. Classroom behavior and other non-academic measures "were weaker in 2001 than before the Challenge." And even the schools that did show meaningful improvement couldn't be consistently replicated within the Challenge districts themselves, let alone around the nation.

In an odd quirk of history, the Wreck of the Annenberg was foreshadowed by President Clinton during the launch ceremony. Clinton thanked Annenberg for his generosity, and added that the "people in this room who have devoted their lives to education are constantly plagued by the fact that nearly every problem has been solved by somebody somewhere, and yet we can't seem to replicate it everywhere else." Clinton would go on to explain that the most pressing need in American education is "to have a system to somehow take what is working and make it work everywhere. Nobody has unraveled this mystery."

Obama is now asking voters for the power to waste hundreds of billions of taxpayer dollars.

Clinton was half right. The lack of a mechanism for automatically replicating excellence is indeed the most pressing problem in American education. The absence of such a mechanism is what doomed the Annenberg Challenge from the start. Clinton's mistake was believing that the mystery hadn't already been solved.

Well before the president's December 1993 speech, a Scottish economist observed that the people of Athens had solved the scaling-up problem in the 5th century B. C. Classical Athenians sought out instruction for their children, and teachers competed for the privilege of serving them. "That demand for instruction produced, what it always produces, the talent for giving it; and the emulation which an unrestrained competition never fails to excite appears to have brought that talent to a very high degree of perfection." The economist in question was of course Adam Smith.

A careful reading of *The Wealth of Nations* was not the only way to discover that markets of competing schools automatically disseminate effective practices. A moment's reflection on the meteoric growth of private tutoring firms would have been enough. The Kumon tutoring chain began in Japan in 1954, and had a worldwide enrollment in the millions by the mid 1990s. Today it enrolls 4 million students in 45 countries. In the U. S., Kumon has 1,280 locations and continues to grow rapidly — as do its competitors, such as Sylvan Learning and Huntington.

This for-profit tutoring industry has proven the validity of Adam Smith's analysis: parent-driven educational marketplaces provide incentives that automatically encourage the replication of effective models, just as they ensure the freedoms that allow such replication to take place.

Monopolistic public-school systems lack these necessary incentives and freedoms, and so exemplary public schools remain isolated, and often fizzle out. A 2002 RAND study concluded that model school "reforms need to have rewards and sanctions associated with them." Countless "model schools" efforts had been going on in the public system since the 1960s — all of which lacked market freedoms and incentives, and all of which failed to spark the system-wide transformation that Annenberg sought.

Perhaps the greatest tragedy of the Annenberg Challenge is that years after its failure, many of those who led it at the national and regional level — including Senator Obama — still actively reject the lessons it should have taught them, and indeed that should have already been apparent before it even began. Senator Obama's platform calls for a "blue ribbon panel" to identify "successful programs and innovations across the country that should be scaled" but he explicitly rejects the very market forces essential to the scaling-up process.

Obama's opponent, John McCain, stresses the need to give all parents an easy choice of public and private schools, opening up American education to the freedoms and incentives that have the **proven ability to transform it**. Barack Obama, despite being in the cockpit of the Annenberg Challenge disaster, hasn't yet learned that lesson.

Here now, is a vital point that I would like to add: parents were locked out of these discussions, and once again, the federal sunshine laws were apparently violated.

Now, let me introduce you to another author and academic that can see things as they truly are. Her name is Mary Grabar and she has written dozens of books and articles that have appeared in academic periodicals all across the country. In an article in Media, Grabar points out the complexities of the Ayers/Obama relationship and how Common Core—Obama's nationalized education curriculum—would be dropped like a bomb into American schools. And no one knew the bomb had gone off until their children came home from school

Ms. Grabar's article in AIM September 21, 2012…"Terrorist Professor Bill Ayers and Obama's Federal School Curriculum". Ms. Grabar's article is quite lengthy, so I put emphasis on the most interesting points she makes. You will see the outline of a rather influential silhouette hanging over our children.[25]

TERRORIST PROFESSOR BILL AYERS AND OBAMA'S FEDERAL SCHOOL CURRICULUM

Three years after the Department of Education announced a contest called Race-to-the-Top for $4. 35 billion in stimulus funds, some parents, teachers, governors, and citizen and public policy groups are coming to an awful realization about the likely outcomes:

A national curriculum called Common Core

Regionalism, or the replacement of local governments by federally appointed bureaucrats

---

25   https://www. aim. org/special-report/terrorist-professor-bill-ayers-and-=obamas-federal-school-curriculum/print

A leveling of all schools to one, low national standard, and a redistribution of education funds among school districts

An effective federal tracking of all students

The loss of the option of avoiding the national curriculum and tests through private school and home school

Working behind the scenes, implementing these policies and writing the standards are associates from President Obama's community organizing days. In de facto control of the education component is Linda Darling-Hammond, a radical left-wing educator and close colleague of William "Bill" Ayers, the former leader of the communist terrorist Weather Underground who became a professor of education and friend of Obama's.

When these dangerous initiatives are implemented, there will be no escaping bad schools and a radical curriculum by moving to a good suburb, or by home schooling, or by enrolling your children in private schools.

How was it that 48 governors entered Race-to-the-Top without knowing outcomes?

It was one of the many "crises" exploited by the Obama administration. While the public was focused on a series of radical moves coming in rapid-fire succession, like the health care bill and proposed trials and imprisonment of 9/11 terrorists on domestic soil, governors, worried about keeping school doors open, signed on. Many politicians and pundits praised Obama on this singular issue, repeating the official rhetoric about raising standards.

It stands to reason, though, that education policies would be consistent with Obama's agenda. After all, one of his most controversial associations, highlighted during the 2008 presidential campaign, was with an *education* professor, Bill Ayers. As a terrorist, he and his wife, Bernadine Dohrn, had dedicated their *Prairie Fire Manifesto* to Sirhan Sirhan, the convicted assassin of Robert F. Kennedy. It was for this reason that Kennedy's son, Christopher Kennedy, chairman of the University of Illinois board of trustees, voted against bestowing "professor emeritus" status on Ayers after he retired. "I intend to vote against conferring the honorific title of our university whose body of work includes a book dedicated in part to the man who murdered my father, Robert F. Kennedy," he said.

Grabar continues to outline the connection and collaboration between Ayers and Obama and education reform with the implementation of Common Core. So, where did he go? He didn't go anywhere. He was hiding in plain sight, with many official visits to the White House on education policy. In fact, many people are surprised to learn the extent to which traditional American culture and values were compromised in Common Core, and reduced time on task in the classroom.

In English classes, teachers will reduce the amount of time spent teaching their subject of literature to only 50 percent, and then to 30 percent in high school, a move criticized by education reform professor Sandra Stotsky. Replacing literature will be "informational texts" like nonfiction books, computer manuals, IRS forms, and original documents, like court decisions and the *Declaration of Independence*. Documents, like the *Declaration*, however, are taught in a manner that *downplays* their significance. Overall, students will be losing a sense of a national and cultural heritage that is acquired through a systematic reading of classical literature and study of history.

From my perspective, and I think many academics agree, this constitutes a 'dumbing down' of our students and reducing the time on task. This is not just unfortunate, this is intentional.

Now I want to introduce you to a third academic. Stanley Kurtz. A Harvard graduate with articles and books published over a decade and more. In an article from 2008, Kurtz delves into Obama's most important executive experience. The Chicago Annenberg Challenge. This is the time in modern America and the point where education really began to take a turn for the worse. Academics across America were panicking due to the fact that children were failing. And those failures were reflecting back on the teachers. Something needed to change and be reformed: the entire educational system.

But how? Well, two things would point the way. First was the National Annenberg Challenge, including the Chicago Annenberg Challenge, and then 2) O.B.E. . . Outcome Based Education would be the centerpiece for the Common Core State Standards force fed to America's youth and families.

Kurtz explains how Ayers and Obama rallied hundreds of millions of dollars into a system that had very little success being replicated for the betterment of the children. It was a gold mine for Ayers and a temporary stopping off point for Obama. Ayers was able to funnel hundreds of millions of dollars into urban schools and then lecture to the teachers on how to "Condition the children" into bringing about an outcome A fictional better academic system of education that had no way of succeeding yet could finance Ayers's radical views to the children, and, importantly, put an end to letter grading on tests. Outcomes were the goal, and success was inevitable. Otherwise, the child would not be college ready. The sad part in that system is that about half the students in any class in America will not go to college, and do not need to be college ready.

OBAMA AND AYERS PUSHED RADICALISM ON SCHOOLS
By Stanley Kurtz

Updated September 23, 2008 12:01 am ET

Despite having authored two autobiographies, Barak Obama has never written about his most important executive experience. From 1995 to 1999, he led an education foundation called the Chicago Annenberg Challenge (CAC) and remained on the board until 2001. The group poured more than $100 million into the hands of community organizers and radical education activists.

The CAC was the brainchild of Bill Ayers, a founder of the Weather Underground in the 1960's. Among other feats, Mr. Ayers and his cohorts bombed the Pentagon, and he has never expressed regret for his actions. Barack Obama's first run for the Illinois State Senate was launched at a 1995 gathering at Mr. Ayer's home.

The Obama campaign has struggled to downplay that association. Last April, Sen. Obama dismissed Mr. Ayers as just "a guy who lives in my neighborhood," and "not somebody who I exchange ideas with on a regular basis." Yet documents in the CC archives make clear that Mr. Ayers and Mr. Obama were partners in the CAC. Those archives are housed in the Richard J. Daley Library at the University of Illinois at Chicago and I've recently spend days looking through them.

The Chicago Annenberg Challenge was created ostensibly to improve Chicago's public schools. The funding came from a national education initiative by Ambassador Walter

Annenberg. In early 1995, Mr. Obama was appointed the first chairman of the board, which handled fiscal matters. Mr. Ayers co-chaired the foundations' other key body, the "Collaborative," which shaped education policy.

The CAC's basic functioning has long been known, because its annual reports, evaluations, and some board minutes were public. But the Daley archive contains additional board minutes, the collaborative minutes, and documentation on the group that CAC funded and reflected. The Daley archives show that Mr. Obama and Mr. Ayers worked as a team to advance the CAC agenda.

One unsettled question is how Mr. Obama, a former community organizer fresh out of law school, could vault to the top of a new foundation? In response to my questions, the Obama campaign issued a statement saying that Mr. Ayers had nothing to do with Obama's "recruitment" to the board. The statement says Deborah Leff and Patricia Albjerg Graham (presidents of other foundations) recruited him. Yet the archives show that, along with Mrs. Leff and Ms. Graham, Mr. Ayers was one of a working group of five who assembled the initial board in 1994. Mr. Ayers founded CAC and was its guiding spirit. No one would have been appointed the CAC chairman without his approval.

The CAC's agenda flowed from Mr. Ayer's educational philosophy, which called for infusing students and their parents with a radical political commitment, and which downplayed achievement tests in favor of activism. In the mid-1960's, Mr. Ayers taught at a radical alternative school, and served as a community organizer in Cleveland's ghetto.

In works like "City Kids, City Teachers" and "Teaching the Personal and the Political," Mr. Ayers wrote that teachers should be community organizers dedicated to provoking resistance to American racism and oppression. His preferred alternative? "I'm a radical, Leftist, small 'c' communist," Mr. Ayers said in an interview in Ron Chepesiuk's, "Sixties Radicals," at about the same time Mr. Ayers was forming CAC.

CAC translated Mr. Ayer's radicalism into practice. Instead of funding schools directly, it required schools to affiliate with "external partners," which actually got the money. Proposals from groups focused on math/science achievement were turned down. Instead CAC disbursed money though various far-left community organizers, such as the Association of Community Organizations for Reform Now (or ACORN).

Mr. Obama once conducted the "leadership training" seminars with Acorn, and Acorn members also served as volunteers in Mr. Obama's early campaigns. External partners like the South Shore African Village Collaborative and the Dual Language Exchange focused core on political consciousness, Afrocentricity and bilingualism than traditional education. CAC's in-house evaluators comprehensively studied the effects of its grants on the test scores of Chicago public school students. They found no evidence of educational improvement.

CAC also funded programs designed to promote "leadership" among parents. Ostensibly this was to enable parent to advocate on behalf of their children's education. In practice, it meant funding Mr. Obama's alma mater, the

Developing communities Project, to recruit parents to its overall political agenda. CA records show that board member Arnold Weber was concerned that parents "organized" by community groups might be viewed by school principals "as a political threat." Mr. Obama arranged meetings with the Collaborative to smooth out Mr. Weber's objections.

The Daley documents show that Mr. Ayers sat as an ex-officio member of the board Mr. Obama chaired through CAC's first year. He also served on the board's governance committee with Mr. Obama, and worked with him to craft CAC bylaws. Mr. Ayers made presentations to board meetings chaired by Mr. Obama. R. Ayers spoke for the Collaborative before the board. Likewise, Mr. Obama periodically spoke for the board at meetings of the Collaborative.

The Obama campaign notes that Mr. Ayers attended only six board meetings, and stresses that the Collaborative lost its "operational role" at CAC after the first year. Yet the Collaborative was demoted to a strictly advisory role largely because of ethical concerns, since the projects of Collaborative members were receiving grants. CAC's own evaluators noted that project accountability was hampered by the board's reluctance to break away from grant decisions made in 1995. So even after Mr. Ayer's formal sway declined, the board largely adhered to the grant program he had put in place.

Mr. Ayers is the founder of the "small schools" movement (heavily funded by CAC), in which individual schools built around specific political themes push students to "confront issues of inequity, war, and violence." He believes teacher

education programs should serve as "sites of resistance: to an oppressive system (His teacher-training
programs were also CAC funded.) The point, says Mr.
Ayers in his "Teaching Toward Freedom," is to "teach
against oppression,"

The Obama campaign has cried foul when Bill Ayers
comes up, claiming "guilt by association" Yet the issue here
isn't guilt by association; it's guilt by participation. As CAC
chairman, Mr. Obama was lending moral and financial
support to Mr. Ayers and his radical circle. That is a story
even if Mr. Ayers had never planted a sing bomb 40 years
ago. [End]

This form of Radicalism is not what one might find in the Oxford Standard
Dictionary. Kurz explains that this radicalism is a complete new paradigm
for how children would receive their education. Academics in education
would explain the reality-based consequences of a standardized, national education curriculum where children were no longer individuals, but
rather, part of a collective. As such, they needed to be programmed and
produced, like human widgets; part of machine.

H. G. Goerner

OBAMA'S CHALLENGE
By Stanley Kurtz

September 23, 2008 11:00 AM

The campaign speaks to "Radicalism"

Today, in a piece in the *Wall Street Journal* entitled, "Obama and Ayers Pushed Radicalism On Schools," I offer a report on my research into the archives of the Chicago Annenberg Challenge (CAC), an education foundation once headed by Barack Obama. As I explained in "Chicago Annenberg Challenge Shutdown?" the Richard J. Daley Library of the University of Illinois at Chicago first agreed to grant, then abruptly denied me, access to the files of this foundation. Subsequently, the Daley Library again reversed their decision and made the CAC files available.

As I note in today's *Journal* piece, I've conveyed the gist of my Annenberg findings to the Obama campaign and offered them a chance to respond. In reply, the Obama campaign has sent me an extended "on the record" statement about Obama's role at the Chicago Annenberg Challenge, and about the nature of his relationship with Bill Ayers. I present that statement in its entirety here:

The Annenberg Challenge records only serve to establish clearly that while Barack Obama and Ayers had occasional contact during Obama's 6 years of service on the bipartisan board, they did not work closely together to exchange and develop policy ideas. In fact, as these records show, Ayers attended a total 6 meetings of the Board during the 6 years of Obama's Board service. And, as these same records also demonstrate, the advisory committee that Ayers co-chaired played no operational role whatsoever once the Challenge hired its Executive Director at the end of its first year.

Ayers had nothing to do with Obama's recruitment to the Board. Barack Obama was encouraged to run for Chair by Deborah Leff, with whom he served on another board, recommended by Pat Graham, and elected by the bipartisan founding board members: Susan Crown, Pat Graham, Stanley Ikenberry, Ray Romero, Arnold Weber, and Wanda White.

Barack Obama months ago confirmed that he had contact with Ayers during the course of his foundation work, and he pointed out that "We served on a board together that had Republicans, bankers, lawyers, focused on education". Senator Obama also said earlier this year that Ayers was "not somebody who I exchange ideas with on a regular basis", a fact that is not in any way contradicted by their contact through the Annenberg Challenge which ended 12 years ago, or by any of the Challenge records.

The suggestion that Ayers somehow dominated the policy or direction of the bipartisan Challenge Board, imprinting it with radical views, is absurd. The Annenberg Challenge was funded by Nixon Ambassador and Reagan friend Walter Annenberg. Republican Governor Jim Edgar, who wrote to Walter Annenberg to encourage the creation of the Challenge, joined Mayor Daley to announce the formation of the Challenge and his administration continued to work closely on education reform with the Board. John McCain has praised an initiative funded by the Challenge. The Challenge's work is still carried on today through to the bipartisan Chicago Public Education Fund, which coordinates closely Chicago Public Schools CEO Arne Duncan and Mayor Daley to improve teacher performance and has included such board members as Illinois Republican Party Chair Andrew McKenna.

The Challenge was established to allocate grants targeted to improve student performance and promote teacher training and leadership development in the Chicago Public Schools. One objective of the Challenge was to improve education for the bottom quartile of students attending Chicago Public Schools — whose reading, math, and basic skills scores improved markedly during the years in which the Challenge invested in city schools. Due to the work of the Challenge and the Fund, the number of board certified teachers in Chicago Public Schools has increased by the hundreds.

As is well known, by the time Barack Obama met him, Ayers was a faculty member at the University of Illinois, and he has held the title of 'distinguished scholar' the University of South Carolina for many years — Ayers held both positions at universities while Republican Governors served on their Boards of Trustees. The detestable acts that Ayers committed decades before occurred when Senator Obama was 8 years old and the Senator has condemned them in no uncertain terms.

While I've addressed this statement in the "Radicalism" piece, I'll extend my response here.

Let's first review CAC's initial setup. In the first year, 1995, Obama headed the board, which made fiscal decisions, and

Ayers co-chaired the Collaborative, which set education policy. During that first year, Obama's formal responsibilities mandated close cooperation and coordination with the Collaborative. As board chair and president of the CAC corporation, Obama was authorized to "delegate to the Collaborative the development of collaborative projects and programs . . . to obtain assistance of the Collaborative in the development of requests for proposals . . . and to seek advice from the Collaborative regarding the programmatic aspects of grant proposals." All this clearly involves significant consultation between the board, headed by Obama, and the Collaborative, co-chaired by Ayers.

From my point of view it is clear that Obama and Ayers needed to coordinate and collaborate on the CAC initial set-up over a period of months. And this is where they developed a friendly political relationship. Common Core is just one of several radical "Changes" we would see during Obama's time as President. It was in 2008 October just before he took office that we see the financial downturn in America take place due to the housing bubble burst.

There were several legislative actions that Obama put in place during his administration and they changed the landscape dramatically . . . forever. He was able to generate Trillions of dollars in TARP money to hand out to survivors and States that were insolvent.

1. 2011 Obama put the Mortgage system on waivers and Fannie Mae and Freddie Mac are now nationalized and in the government's pocket. The former CEO Mr. Franklin Raines walked away from Fannie Mae with an enormous multi-million-dollar package. He was Bill Clinton and Obama's Mortgage czar.
2. With Common Core State Standards, Obama nationalized the Education system.

3. Obama's Affordable Care Act, which is actually nothing more than Socialized medicine.
4. Obama's executive order 13603 March 16, 2012 . . . The National Defense Resources Preparedness Act. This executive order put All of America's Resources under Federal Control in case of a natural disaster (and in small print) "Peace Time" if necessary. When I say under Federal CONTROL of all resources, I do mean ALL resources. First responders, including police and fire fighters; medical personnel and medical supplies; agriculture and food stuffs and the production of same; fresh potable water, waterways, tributaries, and aqueducts, as well as the management and distribution of same. And, in addition, the final and most important resource: labor. "Labor." Control of Labor as a resource. Karl Marx saw labor as the foremost resource for all wealth.

It was Obama's goal to transform the American landscape dramatically, per his Agenda. He needed to convince the American people that it was the rich, the corporations, and the Republicans, who were responsible for them being poor and disenfranchised. He was the embodiment of "hope." He would change all this if they voted for him. Well, they certainly did. Obama won 365 electoral votes in 2008, second only to Roosevelt's landslide in 1936.

Believe it or not, he came well prepared. Obama had a mentor and play book. Years before, in the mid-fifties, Saul Alinsky, the great community organizer, was setting the tone, and creating the course that would be revealed as the bully-pulpit for Obama to appeal to the masses, creating a clear and unobstructed run for the White House, and with it, more government control and intrusion. Obama was articulate, well-educated and smooth. And he knew just how to convince the people that "Fundamental Transformation" would be good for all. Obama made many Americans feel good about government and its role in our lives for the first time in a long time. But this soon became more of the same old rhetoric. Promises not kept, more government intrusion and more division among the politicians and the people.

As the sweeping scale of his societal vision came more clearly in to view, the "change" that he talked about so confidently on the campaign trail began to scare some citizens, and lead to uncomfortable questions about trade-offs. Many in the 'fly over states' were getting raked over the emotional coals, so to speak, and the country became increasingly more divided. For some, the pain increased dramatically, and for many the pain, though mild, simmered and simmered and simmered.

One particular point that bears emphasis is how emotions and feelings have trumped facts and reality on the left. Our young people today are getting "feelings" or "emotions" confused with "facts." Our children's (and many adults') feelings on certain issues have begun to override the practical realities of how these issues are actually addressed. We begin to see children taking issue with parents' positions as "parents"—meaning, adults with authority. We begin to see parents being marginalized in the home by the liberal agenda for the sake of "social warriors" and even teachers hawking the notion that parents were the problem.

For instance, recently there have been spots on television announcing the "tribal" mentality that "it takes a village" to raise a child. On MSNBC, a young lady named Melissa Harris-Perry had her own show, and in one gleaming moment of insight, she professed the belief that our children really do not belong to us. They belong to "the village that raises them." She goes on to explain that we send our children out to school, then to daycare, then at the end of the day they come home, eat dinner, go to bed, and the next morning they are gone again. "It takes a Village to raise a child."

What Ms. Perry chooses to omit is that "we" pay to send our children out to get an education, or take responsibility for home schooling. We pay the daycare centers to watch our children so that we can operate as a family unit, if we don't care for them ourselves. We are seeing more and more how our school and government agencies are challenging long held beliefs about the role of family and faith. In the efforts by the Liberal/ Marxist Machine here in America and our schools, we are seeing "social engineering" take the place of classical education. Parental control over our children is largely being subjugated and transferred to teachers and government agencies. By manipulating children to be more "Politically Correct" and more "Socially Just," we find that often our children's concepts and views have been shaped by the Marxist ideology to challenge authority in defiant ways, and differ dramatically with traditional parental practices. Political and social views, collectivist values and discontent enter the home, followed by strife as our children no longer feel the bond of the love for the family unit. It is truly frightening. Be warned: the information you are about to encounter may shock you.

In the forthcoming article, author Nancy Thorner reveals some of the troubling "engineering" taking place with our children. But first, I will expose an enormously insidious and sinister component of the Liberal / Marxist Machine, which is to systematically dissolve the bond between child and parent. This is pursued, today in our country, using new education processes specifically designed to marginalize the parent in the eyes of the child, and for all intents and purposes, psychologically distance our children from us while emphasizing the good of the collective society.

"THE SMOKING GUN."

Every teacher is provided a "Primer" which guides them through the daily program determined by the Common Core States Standards initiative. There are only a few corporations that print these guides for the teachers working with the federal program that designed CCSS. The curriculum requires certain text be built in, which includes specific psychological tasks to be performed during the daily instruction, to bring about a specific outcome.

Only a handful of corporations print and produce these guides for the teachers. First there is Pearson publishing, which is global in scale, followed by Cengage, McGraw-Hill, and Houghton. There are a few others, but the lion's share of primers are produced by a select few companies already in place. At the same time however, there are local companies that can take the federal guidelines and produce and print the primers for teachers in their immediate area. This is the case in Massachusetts, for instance, where Zaner-Bloser has produced a primer that, like many across the nation, are designed specifically to bring about a belief or behavioral outcome. Rather than having the child spend time on task "learning" ...i.e. absorbing and understanding the significance of information laid out in say, their history books, these primers are set up to ensure that teachers influence the attitudes and beliefs of children, as measured by the responses to in-class prompts and homework exercises. There are primers for math, history, and, in this case ELA. English Language Arts.

Recently, I discovered information about an ELA Zaner-Bloser primer that an inquisitive parent took the time to thoroughly examine, and for our benefit, showed just exactly how the primer is designed and built to ever-so-subtly, yet effectively, marginalize the parent. I cannot stress how important this particular "marginalization" is to the agenda of the Marxist dialectic. This marginalization of the parental authority and eventual dissolving of the bond is crucial in pulling the child away from the parent, so that the "transformation" can take place.

This marginalization of the parent required by the Machine is so sinister, and so destructive in its very nature, its ultimate outcome almost defies description. When I apply just a moment's thought to the intended results of this instruction-- the breaking of the family bond in order for the child to pledge allegiance to the collective-- my mind begins to spin with the horror of what could be.

The parent who discovered this psychological distortion and the engineering of these primers for first graders (yes, first graders), explains in detail how the course is designed to move these young, fresh minds towards a more "Socially Just Society". Yes, that's what is happening to these beautiful babies. Today's children are being taken down a road where societal concepts----"Social Justice", "Social Advocacy" and "Societal Issues" -- that some would argue are age-inappropriate for a six-year-old—are *central* to the instruction and learning. These precious young minds are being taught from the very early grades that our society is inherently unfair and needs their input and advocacy. It doesn't matter that they are barely seven years old. Their Society needs them. Their advocacy will make a difference.

If you think that I am somehow exaggerating, do a web search of "ELA indoctrination by Common Core."

https://www.youtube.com/watch?v=rGph7QHzmo8

This is, without a doubt, The Smoking Gun.

In my experience, the primary concerns of a six year old are food and playtime. But the organized school system under CCSS becomes a new and stressful paradigm, where predetermined attitudes and behaviors are shaped early. This is not right. In my view, the less stress we place on them the better. They will have enough stress placed on them later in life. Let's not complicate the hell out of their lives at the tender age of six.

This new CCSS program is so problematic and so warped, that if these young children are anything like most kids at that age, by the end of the day, they will be so screwed up with visions of some societal duty that they will not be getting the single most important thing that they came there for: An Education. They will be getting an Indoctrination.

For more on precisely how this takes place, and the manner in which schools are essentially transferring the control once exercised by the parent, let's now examine the writings of Nancy Thorner on Social Engineering.

SOCIAL ENGINEERING—TRANSFERRING PARENTAL
CONTROL OF CHILDREN TO TEACHERS
CHILDREN IN OUR PUBLIC SCHOOLS ARE BEING
PUMMELED WITH POLITICAL CORRECTNESS.

By Nancy J. Thorner, January 24, 2018

Children in our public schools are being pummeled with
political correctness. Specific assignments and class discussions are designed purposely to promote specific political viewpoints which may seriously oppose those of their
parents. This new political correctness is carefully woven
through textbooks and classroom assignment starting in
kindergarten and reaches its apex in college.

Guilt plays a huge part in the indoctrination process as emphasis is on the group, not the individual. This is necessary
so future generations will be prepared to "work" together
in their communities and follow instructions which may
oppose those in power. Individual thinking will be carefully controlled. In addition, in many schools today, the
children are required to fill a certain number of hours of
community service so as to qualify for their diploma. In a
Sustainable world, proper attitude is at least as important
as scholarship.

To understand why social engineering in our public schools
is happening, it is necessary to be aware of Agenda 21 and
Sustainable Development and how the implementation of
these United Nations authored programs is being felt in
many areas of our life.

Earth Summit of 1992 and Agenda 21

Sustainable Development was first conceived by the Brundtland Commission, chaired by Gro Harlem Brundtland, the Vice President of the World Socialist Society. The term was first brought to the Secretary General of the United Nations, Maurice Strong, a staunch supporter of Communist China, but it was the 1992 Earth Summit which resulted in Agenda 21 and a drastic new strategy for sustainable development. It was signed by 178 world leaders including President George H. W. Bush. Agenda 21 proposes an array of actions with the U.N.'s 1,000-page report, and strategy for sustainable development, which are intended to be implemented by every person on Earth, and which calls for specific changes in the activities of all people, especially those in the United States. The proposed changes will be realized by most every American and will be applied to most every aspect of our lives.

The Agenda 21 educational curriculum, to ensure proper citizenship, is known as Common Core and is intended to be "life-long." Read here to see the U.N. Agenda 21 priorities for elementary classroom curriculum. Quite telling is Priority 3, "Foster Global Citizenship," which is explained as follows:

> "The world faces global challenges, which require global solutions. These interconnected global challenges call for far-reaching changes in how we think and act for the dignity of fellow human beings. It is not enough for education to produce individuals who can read, write and count. Education must be transformative and bring shared values to life. It must cultivate an

active care for the world and for those with whom we share it."

Accordingly, an emphasis on Social Justice is being taught in schools to foster the Global goal of Agenda 21. Thus, Social Justice has become an integral part of how children are being taught to think and act as outlined in Common Core curriculum.

What is Social Justice?

Social justice can be described as the right and opportunity for all people "to benefit equally from the resources afforded us by society and the environment." But life doesn't pretend to be fair. If it were, there would not be some born with inferior intelligence, financial instability, or with an unappealing physical appearance. Those who are among the more fortunate are those born in America, where all are given equal opportunities and success is based on work ethics and perseverance.

An article by Selwyn Duke in the New America dated Wednesday, December 27, 2018, exposed a middle school in Wisconsin that was caught brainwashing students with a "Privilege Test." The article relates how, after reading *To Kill a Mockingbird*, 150 eighth-graders at West Bend's Badger Middle School (an area primarily blue collar), were asked to check boxes next to statements that applied to them, such as "I feel comfortable in the gender I was born in," "I never doubted my parents' acceptance of my sexuality," "I have never been called a derogatory term for a homosexual," "I have never been told that I'm attractive for my race," and "I have never been called a terrorist."

Although the school has discontinued the survey, it didn't exactly issue a mea culpa, although it had been using this survey for years.

American Thinker's Thomas Lipson offered these reflections for the lack of contrition by Badger Middle School Principal Dave Uelman:

"The educrats believe it is their duty to enlighten the vulnerable young minds whose care has been entrusted to them by the state"—and who otherwise would be subject to the guidance of only their yahoo parents.

Lifson continues, "Adolescence is a time of identity formation for adulthood, and is full of insecurity and pain, hard enough without being pushed into thinking of yourself as the guilty victimizer of people you've never met." "Guilt" is the operative word; this school exercise is merely a reflection of "white privilege" theory, which in recent years has swept academia.

Teacher as purveyors of culture and tolerance?

Michele Hernandez, author of Social Justice Projects in the Classroom / Edutopia, stated in her article the belief that vulnerable young minds should be entrusted to teachers as educators.

> "As educators, we're charged with preparing our students to be successful in life and productive members of society. But with all the focus on standardized tests and core curriculum, we've forgotten that the concept

of literacy should also include culture and tolerance of diverse people and backgrounds."

"One of the best ways to develop cultural literacy and help our students understand these goals is through social justice processes and projects, activities that develop a mindset of concern for our society's inequity in wealth, education, and privilege. These projects empower our students to effect change through awareness, advocacy, activism, and aid."

Although these statements sound appealing, and it would be wonderful if everyone could experience success, everyone will not do so, because we are not robots that can be programmed for a desired outcome. Also, each of us is uniquely different and that fact must be celebrated, rather than obscured.

Should Schools be Involved in Social Engineering?

Parents must investigate whether social engineering exists in their schools. They can discover this in various ways, without asking directly the teacher or authorities, most of whom are either unwilling or prohibited from answering. The following are suggestions for parents:

Is the school using Common Core material? If so, there is likely cause for concern.

Carefully check homework assignments for material you find unusual or different than you experienced.

Ask your young child if the teacher spends a great deal of time talking about harmony, fairness, and equality.

Common Core curriculum often consists of material that challenges children's actions and beliefs, without concern if they conflict with their family's opinions on such matters. The emphasis is on the World rather than our own country, and thus patriotism is not only under-emphasized; it is often discouraged. Common Core material emphasizes all that is global rather than American. It is a precursor to a one-world-government.

Social-engineering schemes are largely foisted upon our children. Is this really the school's domain, when they should be teaching children the skills needed to function in society and ultimately be successful in a job? Skills such as reading and writing are not given the same amount of time previous generations enjoyed as these new concepts are emphasized instead.

Parents are now asking important questions previous generations never considered. Why are more students graduating from high school today but not ready for college? Why are many students testing below average in their ability to read and write? Are teachers qualified to teach the difference between right and wrong? Isn't this more the responsibility of parents, rather than the state that has been seduced into following the dictates of the U.N. in its goal of establishing a "one-world-government"? It is time for parents and the public to ask these questions with the expectation of receiving honest answers.

Sadly, the one place we thought our children would be safe to grow and prosper may be the very place which demands more careful investigation for usurping the role of parents.[end]

Ms. Thorner goes on to describe the very specific alienation families feel, and details the assault on our children perpetrated by the Marxist/Ayers Machine. She identifies the way in which parents are becoming marginalized in America for the sake of globalism and are somehow becoming seen as the problem. This 180-degree shift in direction for our educational systems is truly dangerous, as it erodes the power of the parent and favors allegiance to the collective.

I invite you to closely read this next excerpt from author Berit Kjos. In her book, Brave New Schools, she outlines many of the enormous educational reforms going on at the United Nations and UNESCO, funneling down into the American educational system.

BRAVE NEW SCHOOLS, CHAPTER 2,
THE INTERNATIONAL AGENDA

"[A] major goal . . . should be . . . to organize a worldwide education program . . . in the process, we should actively search for ways to promote a new way of thinking about the current relationship between human civilization and the earth." Al Gore, *The Earth in the Balance*

"The basic goal of education is change—human change . . ." Harold Drummon, former president of the Association for Supervision and Curriculum Development (ASCD)

"Enlightened social engineering is required to face situations that demand global action now . . . Parents and the general public must be reached also, otherwise, children and youth enrolled in globally oriented programs may find themselves in conflict with values assumed in the home. And then the educational institution frequently comes under scrutiny and must pull back." Professor John Goodlad, Foreword in *Schooling for a Global Age*

> "We can't teach that only America is good," said Seema Desai, a tenth-grader who moved from India to Florida in 1993. "That would hurt my feelings."

Seema had joined an impassioned war—led by the local teachers' union—against three Lake County school board members who wanted Florida schools to emphasize America's unique merits. Seeking to overturn a requirement that would "indoctrinate" students with the intolerable old-paradigm notion that America is best, the union had sued the school board. Such ethnocentric teaching, it argued, emphasizes one culture over another. Therefore, it breaks a state law that requires multicultural education.

Did you know that multiculturalism ruled out loyalty to our country? I didn't. Like most parents, I believed that multicultural education simply helps students understand other cultures and people. In reality, it trains students to view the world and its people from a global and pantheistic perspective rather than from a national and Judeo-Christian perspective. In other words, it is designed to speed *the paradigm shift*—**the current transformation toward a radical new way of thinking, believing, and relating to "our global family.**

This paradigm shift is supposed to prepare students for life in the 21st century "global village," the envisioned worldwide community of people joined together through high-tech superhighways and a common set of values. To mold world-class students, social engineers are testing the latest techniques in behavior modification on our children. As you will see in coming chapters, children must either reject their old home-taught faith or stretch it far beyond biblical boundaries to include the world's pantheistic, polytheistic belief systems.

This very real concept that Kjos speaks of, this paradigm shift, explains what the entire Liberal/Marxist enterprise is geared toward achieving. Let me be more frank: this constitutes theft. This paradigm shift baked in to the instruction is bringing with it the loss of an entire generation of young minds, stealing independence of thought, and dramatically altering moral precepts, lifestyle and society. Mind you, this is merely an excerpt from a much longer dissertation about the international agenda. Please see the book to learn for yourself from Ms. Kjos how social engineering gets intensified by the United Nations and UNESCO. In short, for over forty years the UN has sought to globalize education and normalize collectivism; a one-world association of human beings, achieved by socially engineering our children to fight the ravages of climate change, poverty, hunger and war.

This kind of "Education for All" leads to **global socialism** and not to the kind of freedoms of thought and expression the American republic has offered its people from around the world for centuries. I believe it breeds intolerance and religious persecution, not respect and religious freedom in the tradition of American independence. It produces a pliable workforce that can easily be manipulated, not individuals who stay true to their conscience. It follows the blueprint of Soviet indoctrination, which should come as no surprise considering the secretive Soviet-American educational exchange agreements led by the Carnegie Foundation during the 1980s.[26]

---

26 https://www.chronicle.com/article/higher-education-in-the-80s-some-highlights/

Now, back to emotions for the child. Take for instance homelessness. Our young ones see people out on the streets of our cities, and they get deeply concerned with the issue. They get upset that these people have no home. Yet they cannot understand the reality, when the adults attempt to explain, that much of what the child is seeing is brought about by drug use, mental issues, or, in many cases, the lack of taking personal responsibility. Their feelings about the plight of homeless adults can be used as more fuel for collective, not personal, responsibility.

Here are two additional points made by Dr. Thomas Sowell:

> "Emotions neither prove nor disprove facts. There was a time when any rational adult understood this. **But years of dumbed-down education, an emphasis on how people feel, have left too many people unable to see through the media gimmick.**"

> "The problem isn't that Johnny can't read. The problem isn't even that Johnny can't think. The problem is that Johnny doesn't know what thinking IS. He confuses it with Feelings."

As we move deeper into the uncharted waters of public school instruction at home to limit the impacts of COVID-19, with mass distance-learning relying upon web-based lessons becoming the norm, I invite you to envision the next few years looking through this lens. While it is certainly true that the social and emotional needs of young people must be understood and addressed—especially during this pandemic—does it require a team of school staff? Might the parents and other family members play a critical role in building resilience? Or perhaps are we willing to trust our "brave new schools" and the collectivist curricula as they march ahead.

4

The Method

Around the turn of the twentieth century, John Dewey was an acclaimed educator and had convinced many policy makers that our system of education was in need of major reform. A considerable amount of Dewey's efforts went into social reform through Education, and many policy makers during that era supported his views.

Dewey saw our schools as the perfect place to begin a child's education, especially advocating for social, political and cultural transformation. In Chicago, Illinois, at the University of Chicago, Dewey was able to acquire grants for classroom labs to study the influence of "Critical Pedagogy" on children as young as seven years old. In 1919, he founded the New School for Social research in New York and in 1896 he started the University of Chicago Laboratory Schools to study, apply and test his socialist/progressive ideas on young students and see firsthand the results of his pedagogical methods.

Critical Pedagogy was spawned from "Critical Theory," and its premise was to indulge students in social and political activism and teach them through self-actualization, that they could bring about social, political and economic change. It was a call to action by Dewey to inform the students, and ultimately the masses, that America had several historically and present day "Severely Flawed Elements" within its system. These flaws were racism, sexism and capitalism, and they needed to be condemned and removed.

Dewey was not alone in this endeavor either. George S. Counts was a big proponent of "social reconstructionism." Most everyone reading this book can figure out that premise.

These two gentlemen along with many others were the forerunners to Ayers's bloodless cultural revolution. They were all members, in one way or another, of predominant socialist parties, right here in America.

Today, there are dozens and dozens of thriving socialist parties that see America as it is now as a detriment to mankind. Oppressive, racist, sexist, unjust, and white privileged! And they are out there getting stronger and gathering momentum. Here's a list of just a few socialist parties in America, bent on her transformation. This is just a handful, however, be aware, there are many devout socialist organizations in this country. Also be aware that there are literally hundreds of liberal Marxist organizations in America today that hide behind an altruistic banner. They profess to be looking out for the disenfranchised, when in fact they are funded by wealthy Marxists across the globe.

1. DSA – Democratic Socialists of America, Bernie's Buddies (but he denies it)
2. ALP – American Laborers Party, an offshoot of Lenin's grassroots party, but smaller
3. SPA – Socialist Party of America
4. SAP—Socialist Alternative Party
...and list goes on and on.

Now let me introduce you to my favorite socialist, Saul Alinsky. Mr. Alinsky gave rise to the Bill Ayers we now know. His "Rules for Radicals" actually set the stage for Ayers's assault on American values, and believe it or not, Mr. Alinsky has another progeny: Barack Obama… and still a third: Hillary Rodham-Clinton.

Alinsky was the original neighborhood gangster. The organizer of the poor and oppressed in the disadvantaged communities of Chicago, Detroit and Cleveland. I could go on for hours, but I will leave you with several tidbits of information that will spark your interest to research for yourself this "organizer."

First, Saul Alinsky patterned his methodology after Vladimir Lenin, "Workers of the world Unite!" He went directly to the poor, disenfranchised and unemployed in these urban communities and told them essentially to "rise up and demand a seat at the table, you must be able to express your concerns from your point of view from down where you are." He urged them to voice their concerns directly and forcefully to local elected officials and others in power. Alinsky made no bones about how the American system purposely left out the voices of the poor in decision-making that would directly affect them. Yet, he never told them that their voices were being heard when they voted, or that they could contact their elected officials as citizens at any time—even their congressmen.

Second, Alinsky would not commit to any ideology or allegiance to any political party. He would not let anyone pin him down, left or right. Here's the best part: Hillary Rodham dedicated her college thesis to Alinsky in qualifying for her bachelor's degree from Wellesley.

Third, both Rodham-Clinton and Obama got their feet wet with Alinsky "Community Organizing" and which led to [obviously] bigger and better liberal political methods and outcomes. Community organizing is grass roots organizing directed at the poor and disenfranchised. It is designed to stir up emotions and perpetuate action by those communities to demand their rights and what they are entitled to. Hillary saw America as a place that promised certain things, and she and Barack both let "The People" know that they deserved this, that they were entitled to these things. A quality of living higher than anywhere else on the planet; an education of the highest order. And that their government can supply these things if they vote for Her / Him.

Fourth, Alinsky was interviewed by William F. Buckley in the early '70s and Alinsky said, quote, "I'd steal before I'd take charity."[27] From where I sit, this does nothing but make a thief out of a person who is hungry. Moreover, Alinsky goes on to talk about "Power." Alinsky said, "All Power is Taken." This is the Liberal/Marxist mindset. Alinsky does not acknowledge the phrase from our constitution which states that power is appointed or granted. It is by 'The consent of the governed' that power is obtained. The Marxist view of power is that it must be seized, by force. The "Revolutionary's" only way of gaining real power is through force, as they understand it.

Fifth—finally and most importantly—the "Ends Justify the Means." Alinsky was a proponent of this ideal. In his 1967 interview with William F. Buckley he is heard to say, "Ethical considerations should never be allowed to interfere with success." Anyone can understand that point . . . and the Liberal/Marxist Machine understands its potential; the ends justify the means.

The Ends?? The White House.

The Means?? By any means necessary.

When people refuse to consider ethics in their pursuit of achieving success, these people are a threat to civil society. This Liberal/Marxist anthology is the number-one play out of the Marxist handbook, but neither Hillary nor Obama could deliver. Dr. Thomas Sowell puts it succinctly:

"When you want to help people, you tell them the Truth. When you want to help yourself . . . you tell the people what they want to hear."[28]

---

27 **Firing Line** with William F. Buckley, Guest Saul Alinsky, (1967). Hoover Institution, Stanford University. https://www.youtube.com/watch?v=M6ybDKaOlvg

28 *Thomas Sowell (2011). "The Thomas Sowell Reader"*, p.398, Basic Books

Now, we dig even deeper into a method that was crucial to developing a child that Ayers could rely upon to carry the banner of social justice, dissent and revolution in America.

OBE. "Outcome-Based Education" has a goal which is self-evident: Outcome Based. And there is actually a more accurate and honest term for this Educational Reformation.

It's called "Operant Conditioning."

But let me take a back seat and once again introduce you to a very intelligent fellow named O. Jerome Brown. Mr. Brown was a teacher in the State of Washington and, after careful consideration, turned his sights on OBE and how it was influencing teaching methods and curriculum across America in the 1990s.

This form of New Age education along with the most influential players: Dewey, Counts, Ayers, Obama, and hundreds of other players (pointed out by Kurtz, Grabar, and Coulson) hidden in the maze of Government bureaucracy; is by design, pointing the children-- our children—toward a world that will extinguish a white political hierarchy. Establish a classless society. Install a centralized governing system of controls that will usher in A New World Order to bring about Robert Muller's ideal of a world with **. . . No Hunger . . . No Poverty . . . and No War.**

This ideal world of Robert Muller's is far from reality today however. In a World where all people are free, his ideal can only be established by a total and complete set of worldwide controls. Let Mr. Jed Brown explain the methodology. Jed Brown digs deep into Operant Conditioning to unveil a complete system of conditioning techniques designed to bring about an outcome. An outcome which produces a viable labor resource, capable of delivering what is needed for society and "Sustainable Development."

THE SKINNER BOX SCHOOL

"The 'Skinner-Box' School" by Jed Brown was published in the March 1994

Outcome-Based Education (OBE) has become a blight on the landscape of our national heritage. After only a few years of OBE, whole school systems are beginning to wither and die. Much worse, the children, their minds once fertile fields of intellectual soil, are even now being infected by the worm of ignorance. True learning is starved to death, as all of the nutrients of sound academic practice are being replaced with a dust-bowl curriculum that is structured to secure proper attitudes for the "Brave New World." Sadly, the only "outcome" of OBE will be a baser society, a society in which the nobility of the mind is lost to the savagery of enslavement.

But wait! Parents have been told that Outcome-Based Education has nothing to do with changing the attitudes and values of their children; that OBE will improve learning for all children through "best-practices" research. What parents are not being told is that the research base for OBE is from the field of psychology, not education; that in psychology, the term "learning" is synonymous with the term "conditioning." What parents are not being told is that Outcome-Based Education is not education at all; it is but the hollow substitute of psychological conditioning or, as it is sometimes called, behavior modification.

Why is conditioning replacing the teaching/learning process in our schools? If the object is to change the attitudes and values of the young, why would "behavior modification" be used? Why not work with attitudes and values directly? Just tell the children what they must believe! After

all, the conventional wisdom is that attitudes control behavior. If a child develops the "right" attitudes, he will behave in the "right" manner. Beyond the fact that parents
would not stand for such an intrusion as an overt assault
on traditional values, psychologists know something that
lay people do not. They realize that the direct approach to
changing values does not work.

Modern psychological research suggests that the opposite of conventional wisdom is true. It is our behavior that
shapes our attitudes, not the other way around. Therefore,
to control a child's attitudes and values, it is first necessary
to modify the child's behavior. If the child has the "right"
behavior, then his attitude will change to accommodate the
behavior; his value system will change to reflect his new
set of attitudes. It is like falling dominoes: if the first piece
is toppled, then the rest will tumble after. Thus, conditioning, i.e. modifying behavior, is the perfect method for
instilling in children the new value system required of
citizen of the New World Order. Our schools know that
changing behavior is the first domino. Remember, "the
student shall demonstrate."

To understand the devastation of OBE conditioning, it is
important to know its origins and how it is being used to
change children forever. The lineage of psychological conditioning can be formally traced back to the early part of
this century, to an American psychologist named John B.
Watson. Watson is credited as the father of the Behaviorist
School of Psychology. He believed that psychology should
become the science of behavior, discarding references
to thoughts, feelings, and motivation. For Watson, only
that which was observable was important. The goal of

psychology, he thought, should be to predict a behavioral response given a particular stimulus.

Further, it was a time of great debate in psychology. The debate centered on whether heredity or the environment had the most profound effect on the development of the individual. Watson believed that heredity had little or no effect, that a person's development was almost totally dependent upon his environment. In fact, Watson boasted,

"Give me a dozen healthy infants, well formed, and my own specified world to bring them up in, and I'll guarantee to take any one at random and train him to become any type of specialist I might select—doctor, lawyer, artist, merchant-chief, and yes, even beggar-man and thief, regardless of his talents, penchants, tendencies, abilities, vocations, and race of his ancestors."

Watson's statement is at the heart of OBE: Watson became the most influential force in spreading the idea that human behavior was nothing more than a set of conditioned responses. According to the narrow view of Behaviorism, learning is nothing more than "a relatively permanent change in an organism's behavior due to experience." Other psychologists first, then educational leaders, and finally rank-and-file teachers have been persuaded to adopt the Behaviorists' view of education. The richness of education is thus lost, as the schooling experience is reduced to only applied learning. No longer does learning enhance the internal focus of man—it is but an external shell. The curriculum has become hollow and learning has become mere conditioning.

Three different types of psychological conditioning have invaded schools with Outcome-Based Education and education reform. Each type has its specified purpose in controlling the behavior, and therefore the minds, attitudes, and values of our young. The first is Classical Conditioning, developed by a Russian physiologist named Ivan Pavlov only a few years before Watson's conception of Behaviorism. The second, credited to B. F. Skinner, is Operant or Instrumental Conditioning. The third, attributed to Albert Bandura, is Observational Learning. Each of these Behaviorist conditioning approaches is woven through the OBE reforms of education to accomplish only one thing: to control attitudes by controlling behavior.

Classical, or Pavlovian Conditioning, can be defined as creating a relatively permanent change in behavior by the association of a new stimulus with an old stimulus that elicits a particular response. Working on physiology experiments, Pavlov noted that each time the dogs he used as subjects were to be fed, they began to salivate. He identified the food as the "old" stimulus and the salivation as the response, or behavior. Pavlov rang a bell each time the food was presented to the dogs. The bell was identified as the "new" stimulus. After several pairings of the bell and the food, he found that the dogs would salivate with the bell alone. A change in behavior had occurred.

All well and good, but what do dogs, food, saliva, and bells have to do with changing attitudes in children? Just like Pavlov's dogs, children's behavior patterns can be changed with Classical Conditioning. Upon sufficient pairings, a child will associate old behavior patterns and consequent attitudes with new stimuli. The Pavlovian approach is therefore a potent weapon for those who wish to change the belief structures of our children. Further, Classical Conditioning may be used to set children up for further conditioning that is necessary for more complex attitude shifts. The method is being used to desensitize children to certain issues that heretofore would have been considered inappropriate for school-age children.

One example of an attitude change by Pavlovian conditioning revolves around the word "family." The term "family," as it is applied to the home setting, is used as the old stimulus. The allegiance to parents and siblings that is normally associated with the term "family" may be thought of as the response, or behavior. With the current education reform movement, the child is told by the teacher that the school class is now the family. Thus, the term "class" may be thought of as the new stimulus. By continually referring to the class or classroom as the family, an attitude change takes place. By association, the child is conditioned to give family allegiance to the class and teacher.

An example of desensitizing children through Classical Conditioning can be seen in the inclusion of gender orientation within the curriculum. The school setting may be thought of as the old stimulus. The formal school setting carries with it a whole set of emotional-behavioral responses, or behaviors. There is an air of authority and legitimacy that is attached to those subjects included in the curriculum. This feeling of legitimacy can be considered a behavioral response. By placing the topic of gender orientation into the curriculum, it is associated with legitimacy of the school settings. Thus, children are desensitized to a topic that is different from the traditional value structure, and hence they are predisposed to further conditioning.

The real meat and potatoes of Outcome-Based Education is Operant Conditioning, or Rat Psychology, so called because B. F Skinner used rats as his experimental subjects. A "Skinner Box," a box containing a press bar and a place to dispense a food pellet, is used to condition the rat to press the bar (the behavior). A food pellet (the stimulus) is used to reinforce the desired behavior, pressing the bar. The rat, having no idea what to expect, is placed in the box. Once in the box, the rat's movements are exploratory and random. As soon as the rat looks towards the bar, the experimenter releases a food pellet. After eating the food, the rat resumes his random movement. Another look, another pellet. Another look, another pellet.

Once the rat is trained to look at the bar, he is required to approach the bar before the pellet is delivered. The rat must then come closer and closer to the bar each time before reinforcement is given. Over time, the rat's behavior is slowly shaped by the experimenter; each trial the rat successively approximates more closely the ultimate behavior of pressing the bar. Eventually the well-conditioned rat will continually press the bar as fast as he can eat. Operant Conditioning is, therefore, defined as a relatively permanent change in behavior by successive approximations through repeated trials using positive or negative reinforcements.

The concept of "successive approximation" is key to understanding the use of Operant Conditioning with Outcome-Based Education. Just as for the rat, the experimenter (the

State) establishes the ultimate goals for children (pressing the bar). OBE requires that specific behavioral outcomes be designed such that the children must master each outcome in succession. The outcomes are designed in a spiral fashion, such that as the child goes further in school, the outcomes more closely approximate the ultimate goals. As children master an outcome, the reinforcement is found in approval (food pellets). Another outcome, more approval. Another outcome, more approval (successive approximation). When the Skinner Box experiment is complete, our children, like rats, will dance to the tune of the State.

Observational Learning, although it does not carry the name conditioning, has been described by Dollard and Miller as a special case of Operant Conditioning. It is Operant Conditioning applied to social behavior. Observational Learning is the twenty-five-cent word for modeling. There are two purposes for Observation Learning in the schools. First, it is a method used to condition a host of social behaviors, like parenting styles, gender roles, problem-solving strategies, and discipline boundaries, Second, it is used as reinforcer of the behaviors and attitudes previously conditioned with Classical and Operant Conditioning.

According to Observational Learning, people model the behavior of those within their "reference groups." Under normal conditions, the child's primary reference group is the family. Nevertheless, children are being conditioned with Classical methods to shift allegiance to their new school family, their new reference group. Once the new group is established, schools use surveys to gauge attitudes and then orchestrate the conditioning process through Observational Learning. Relying almost exclusively on cooperative learning (group learning), OBE reforms unfortunately use Observational Learning to establish and enforce the proper behaviors and attitudes through peer pressure and a forced "group think" process.

The idea that our schools are not dealing in attitudes and values is ludicrous. The psychologists have ripped the schools from parents and teachers alike. Their only objective is to create children who may look different, but behave the same, think the same, and believe the same. They shall create in each child the "perfect child." Like John B. Watson, they shall create children as they see fit. They shall do it with conditioning, not teaching. Is it any wonder that our schools are failing to educate children when we use rats as the example of exemplary learning? Welcome to the "Brave New World." Welcome to the "SKINNER BOX SCHOOL."

Now that we have considered outcome-based education aimed at the individual and our children, let's look at the positioning of education to advance the collective society and the new global social order, already in the works.

H. G. Goerner

EDUCATION FOR THE NEW INTERNATIONAL SOCIAL ORDER
By D. Jerome (Jed) Brown, August 1995

Education for the New International Social Order is organized under the Complex Life Role of Family Member. This Life Role, however, is not restricted to membership in a traditional nuclear family. The definition of "Family Member" is expanded to include not only the nuclear family, but also the community or "urban village" and the global family of the New World Order.

The Determinants of the Family Member Organizer are Collectivism, Communitarianism and Pacifism. It is through the activities and processes that emanate from these Determinants that children shall be conditioned to behave in accordance with the group norms rather than individual inclinations and to feel involved in the participatory structure of the New World Order.

As an aid to understanding, it is necessary to revisit the theories of Karl Marx. One theory of particular significance is Marx's Theory of Alienation. As may be remembered from the May edition of this publication, Marx calculated that all things have an economic foundation, that the very wealthy elite, by controlling the means and relations of productions, oppress the masses, or workers, of the world. Marx further postulated that the masses, as a result of oppression, would begin to feel more and more alienated or isolated. This alienation, according to Marx, would eventually become so great that the masses would revolt against the elite oppressors and create a truly classless society. This revolution would bring an end to the elite class.

2

The elite do not wish to lose control. It, therefore, becomes easy to see that Marx, in formulating his theory, identified the great dilemma of the elite. This very real dilemma is summed up in the questions, "How do we (the elite) maintain control over the masses, oppress them for our gain, and at the same time keep them from feeling so alienated or isolated that they revolt against us?" The first half of the equation is child's play for the elite. By virtue of their wealth, they simply set about constructing a New International Economic Order and a New International Governmental Order. These two new orders maintain the elite's control and create a slave workforce for their multinational corporations. However, the second half of the equation is considerably more difficult. These elite must also restructure the entire society to lessen the isolation of the masses and, thus, avert a revolution.

The restructuring of a society is no easy task, but there is a road map for them to follow. To begin to see the route to be taken and destination of the journey, there is at least one other scholar of the past that must be understood, the French political philosopher, Jean-Jacques Rousseau. Encapsulated, Rousseau believed that man is basically good and that his tendency toward violence is due to the inability of the common man to emotionally deal with complex situations. If the revolution spoken of by Marx is to be averted, then it is the noble obligation of the elite, who consider themselves evolutionarily advanced, to restructure society in accordance with Rousseau's dictum. Therefore, the elite have decided that although the New International Governmental Order shall be global rule by Democratic Centralism, the New International Social Order shall be full cooperative involvement within small, egalitarian, collectively organized communities—THINK GLOBALLY, ACT LOCALLY!!!

Given the Rousseauean orientation of the New International Social Order, it is important to condition children to accept that their sphere of activity should be limited to their own community and that the needs, wants, and desires of each individual must be subjugated to those of the community at large. Therefore, the primary Determinant of the restructured school program is Communitarianism. According to *Webster's Ninth New Collegiate Dictionary*, "Communitarian" is defined as being, "of or related to social organization in small cooperative, particularly collectivist communities." Communitarianism therefore establishes a society comprised of many individual, self-contained communities established under the group norms. The most noteworthy examples of Communitarianism are the Kubbutzim of Israel and the Hippy Communes of the 1960s.

Because Communitarianism, by definition, is partially inclusive of Collectivism, the program model contains some necessarily arbitrary distinctions. Nevertheless, the Frameworks for the school program that flow from the Communitarian Determinant are Shared Decisions, Shared Purpose, Limited Social Base, Equality of Status, Social Responsibility and Group Control. Although some of these Frameworks give rise to structured activities, the conditioning of these behaviors is most generally done through the group process of classroom management. The Conditioning process begins immediately, as classroom facilitators continually refer to the class as the child's family. Through what in psychology is called "paired association learning," the child is conditioned to expand the definition of the nuclear family to include all the members of his class. As the child continues in school, the concept is further expanded to include all students within the school building. The concept is yet further expanded with reference to the community and global family.

After expanding the child's understanding of the term "Family Member," the group process is used to condition the behaviors that will characterize life in the transformed society. A distinction must be made at this juncture between "group process" and "group instruction." Group instruction is a method of the old paradigm, the Disciplined Knowledge Paradigm. It is the instruction of knowledge-based curriculum to several children of similar aptitudes at the same time. The operative phrase is "knowledge-based." Under group instruction, all the children within the group are receiving knowledge from the teacher. "Group Process" is quite a different animal. It is a conditioning technique of the new paradigm, the Lifelong Education Paradigm. It is the facilitation of behavior change within the group setting and has nothing to do with imparting knowledge.

The actual object of the group process, be it used in match, literature, or social studies, is to shape each child's behavior patterns such that over time, those patterns will be consistent with the [Note: is text missing here?] community emphasis of the coming New Social Order. Through the process, children are conditioned to function not as individuals within the entire spectrum of human experience, but as equal members of a group of limited size. They are conditioned to accept that their primary social responsibility is to the group; they share a common purpose and must share equally in the decisions that emanate from that purpose. Ultimately, their behavior is controlled by the group through the rewards and punishments administered by their peers.

The communities of the New Social Order shall be relatively small Collectivist-democratic organizations that cannot be a collection of autonomous individuals, as in the case of the traditional community. In fact, the Collectivist-democratic structure differs greatly from the traditional perspective. For explanation, it is perhaps best to quote from an article by Joyce Rothschild-Whitt entitled, "The Collectivist Organization: An Alternative to Rational-Bureaucratic Models," as found in the August 1979 issue of the American Sociological Review. Ms. Rothschild-Whitt explains:

The collectivist-democratic organization rejects rational bureaucratic justifications for authority. Here authority resides not in the individual, whether on the basis of incumbency in office or expertise, but in the collective as a whole. This notion stems from the ancient anarchist ideal of "no authority," . . . [it is] a process in which all members have the right to full and equal participation. This democratic ideal, however, differs significantly from the conceptions of "democratic bureaucracy" (Lipset et al., 1962), "representative bureaucracy" (Gouldner, 1954) or even representative democracy. In its directly democratic form, it does not subscribe to the established rules of order and protocol. It does not take formal motions and amendments; it does not usually take votes; majorities do not rule and there is no two-party system. Instead, there is a "consensus process" in which all members participate in the collective formulation of problems and negotiation of decision . . . Only decisions which appear to carry the consensus of the group behind them, carry the weight of moral authority.

...The Collectivist-democratic community of the New Social Order cannot exist without congenial relationships and a significant level of group cohesion. To build consensus within the collective, people must get along. Therefore, the third Determinant for education in the New Social Order is Pacifism. To create the necessary docility in society, any aggressive tendencies that children may have are extinguished through the conditioning process. The program Frameworks for Pacifism are Conflict Resolution and Violence Prevention. Although most rational people realize that a society that feeds upon itself in a violent manner cannot long ensure that habits of civil behavior and obedience to the rule of law have traditionally been ingrained through classroom discipline. Nevertheless, the new school programs go beyond that which has traditionally been accomplished through reasonable discipline. The activities and processes of the restructured school are designed to create children who are acquiescent, submissive and compliant within the group setting. These behavioral traits not only preserve the serenity of the collective community but also assure subservience to the global masters of the New World Order.

Now, as Jed Brown so eloquently explains, all things have an economic foundation. Here is the part that the new social order is, by design, so desperately pushing and the Liberal/Marxists are so desperately needing: "Sustainability."

As California is headed for financial collapse, so is the rest of America. This brings into specific relief a huge issue that most seem to kick down the proverbial road. Bankruptcy.

Should California fold, this will start a cascade of worldwide events that will ultimately begin "the re-set." Our federal, state and local debts are unsustainable. When the re-set is in full swing, millions of pensioners elderly and young alike, will feel the pinch of no money to spread around, and more specifically, no government services to be had.

This will be when a World Order must be in place (according to our modern day Marxists) to feed and house the masses. The re-set will mark the culmination of the budgetary system that conservatives have begged for and lived by for centuries, and the Liberals never could adopt. The sad part here is, it could have been prevented, and now, everything and everyone will be controlled; from the time we wake up, to the moment we close our eyes at night. We will begin to see and understand that the liberal tax-and-spend anthem was severely flawed. Conservatives have pushed budgetary constraints since this whole damn thing began. However, the unions and big government forced socially just protections into existence. When all along that protection, that sustainability, should have been up to the individual, not our federal government.

Pioneers from bygone years had no such security. No safeguards built into the systems they lived in. It was men, their wives and children, who considered their entire life a gift, and made something of it; rather than believing they were entitled to it. They lived on strict budgets and saved and worked and pretty soon, they found a dream had come true: Independence, in all its glory.

Free of all encumbrances. Able to determine one's own destiny.

Well, if Americans truly love America the way it is, then it is time to fight to protect America and keep what we have. The Liberal/Marxist Machine wants to bring about the New Social Order to save the world from itself. True Americans, like the pioneers of old, can and will get it done, without this new social order. The Machine can keep the change. Americans can get through anything with the currency they already have: resolve.

5

The Means...The Mainstream Media Harnessed

In the 1960s and 70s, journalists and news-reporting organizations held in the highest esteem that the integrity of whatever they were reporting on would be truthful and honest and without bias.

That integrity has all but been destroyed by ratings and Hate for an America that is seen by Marxist proponents of a New World Order that she has gone from a pillar of strength for the World, to a country whose only redeeming quality is that it pays billions in welfare dollars, and will provide it to virtually anyone who applies.

And here are the means by which these protagonists of dissent have resorted to: ratings and enormous quantities of money. Because the more dollars the mainstream media (MSM) can generate, the more air-time can be purchased to "condition" the viewers. The Liberal/Marxist Machine in America consists of thousands of journalists in today's MSM that because of money and ratings have become nothing more than propagandists. Sensationalism (blood) and a politically correct narrative.

But that scenario is only a very small part of the paradigm shift that we are witnessing.

We are also witnessing an enormous swath of viewers being pulled to the left by networks that lean left, and some that lean far left. CNN, ABC, CBS, NBC, MSNBC, PBS, USA Today, Google News. The list accounts in total for roughly 23 liberal national news outlets. Fox is one of a very few conservative outlets.

With hundreds of millions of viewers watching the liberal biased news and commentary on a daily basis, and with liberal news outlets that spin their version of the truth to the point that truth has become virtually unrecognizable, it's our youth that suck it right up like a sponge.

The number of people that are getting liberal biased information that is in many cases completely dishonest, is frightening. Some estimates put the ratio at 100:1. A hundred [or more] liberal biased news outlets local and national are feeding the public a Liberal/Marxist dialectic propaganda. That ratio accounts for the local, state or city liberal news outlets that inundate the public with left-leaning points of view and a narrative agenda.

For decades the news outlets were set in their position to deliver fair and balanced news. News in an objective unbiased way. Facts with no spin. No embellishment. Today that has changed completely.

This juggernaut is the catalyst with which the Liberal/Marxist Machine has captured and is using to prove to people everywhere that a New America is what is needed. The news outlets for the Machine have enormous influence, resources, wealth, and, above all, enormous coverage. This coverage has an effect on the outcomes of a myriad of topics and more importantly, elections. When the public gets told that a particular candidate is evil and untrustworthy and that information is disseminated throughout the country on a minute by minute basis, the outcome becomes predictable.

Constantly—minute by minute—hour by hour and day by day, the Liberal Machine beats into the minds of the people how America is oppressive, racist, unfair, and unjust. The Liberal/Marxist Machine finds anyone, anyone, even remotely close to that topic, as the cause for America's demise and destruction. The Machine will place blame anywhere other than where it belongs.

Folks across the country and around the world are being inundated with news that is no longer objective news. It's biased propaganda that is bought by huge organizations across the spectrum of publishing networks, predominately liberal, and that have now grown increasingly Marxist.

Let me reference one issue that I cannot get out of my mind: Why do liberals hate the fact that Trump won in 2016? Here's why: Against all odds, he defeated Hillary and The Liberal/Marxist Machine, while millions of loyal Hillary and Marxist subjects were shocked with disbelief for weeks. They absolutely hate the fact that Trump walked in and stole their Seat. And I thought and thought about this for a good while. Is it in their nature to despise losing . . . or is it something deeper?

I discovered that it is much deeper.

Here is my conclusion: Those thousands of loyal subjects I mentioned, they were enormously invested in Hillary. By that I mean dollars. Hundreds and hundreds if not billions of dollars were thrown at her and the future she was to bring about. It is almost certain that Hillary would have sold America out to the higher order for a seat at the head of the global table of power. But the deeper issue at hand is the effect Trump's victory had on those deeply invested in Hillary. When a person of enormous wealth, power and influence makes a bad bet, their power and influence get diminished exponentially. These power players do not have any qualms with buying a $50,000 dollar coat rack. But when they lose at anything, and their money is taken, and they have to watch as it is removed...this infuriates them. Most of all, it makes them look ridiculous. People with tremendous power and influence cannot afford to be made to look ridiculous. Trump's victory made a huge block of Hillary backers . . . LOOK RIDCULOUS.

All the research showed Hillary to be the top contender. The most prepared. The best financed. The first woman as a serious contender for the office of the Presidency, and the Liberal Star!

The Pew Research Institute, part of the Pew Charitable Trust showed numbers that could not be denied. Yet those numbers did not show the soul of America. It didn't show the heart of America. It didn't show the values that make America what it is; individual sovereignty. These are what the Pew numbers did not count.

The single most important element in all of it: the ability of a person to choose their own path. Decide, for themselves, where they want to go. Professor Milton Friedman titled his book with the term "Free to Choose." Mr. Friedman's book has sold millions of copies around the world, but I reference here one very short phrase from this particular book. "Ten years ago, many people were convinced that capitalism, based on free private markets, was a deeply flawed system that was not capable of achieving widely shared prosperity and human freedom. Today conventional wisdom regards capitalism as the only system that can do so."[29]

This single important element is what the mainstream media, Bill Ayers, Obama, Dewey, Dyson and Hillary seem to overlook. Or purposely omit.

Without a strong sense of national sovereignty supported by individual freedoms, which has existed since America was established, not a single Obama or Ayers or journalist would be able to voice their displeasure with the system that encourages dialogue, even when that dialogue is distasteful and arrogant. But in the same breath, if that dialogue is false at its core, our system also encourages the accountability for those lies and prevarications.

America is a country of laws. Whereas before monarchs made the laws and the subjects had no say, today "the consent of the governed" is our most precious precept, and a person's right to choose the most precious ideal. The rule of law is our cornerstone.

And we are on the very precipice of moving so far left that, if it does happen, and a Hillary or Pelosi-type candidate is thrust into the White House as the Liberal/Marxist Machine gets control of the Congress and Senate; there will be an enormous push by the Marxist-minded youth and the Liberal/Marxist inner-city constituents that got them there, to move America into the socialist collective abyss. America will be sold out for her power and resources to the international collective in order to be seated at the head of the global table of power.

---

29 Friedman, M. *Free to Choose: A personal statement*. (1980), Harvest Book – Harcourt, Inc.

This Global Order comes from the mind of Robert Muller. He came to the US in the 1940s and he secured a position at the newly formed United Nations, where he would be a formative highly influential voice for more than four decades. He, until his death in 2010, and the United Nations have been working towards this single ideal since its founding in 1948. And it continues wholeheartedly today.

No Poverty . . . No Hunger . . . No War . . . is the goal.

A wonderful ideal, which can only come about with a total and complete control of every aspect of daily life.

All global resources will go to feeding the world's population. When this is accomplished, you have a workforce unparalleled in consolidation and commitment. If the world's people no longer need to worry and struggle to sustain life, that in and of itself is an enormous selling point to those you wish to have on your side.

All of the world's resources will be trained towards a lifestyle that resembles that of a middle-class American lifestyle. A home, a job, and a living without a struggle. Just commitment to an ideal and fifty hours a week of your labor. Entire communities will spring up overnight. They will house and sustain hundreds of thousands of people within that community. It will be like a large ashram. Travel will be contained within only that community and all needs will be met. ALL needs! No one will need to go outside their community.

Then all resources of a "centralized control network" can be deployed to maintain order. Anyone who dissents will be dealt with. Anyone who takes or covets what does not belong to them will be a liability. Anyone who causes strife of discontentment, will be considered a liability. All liabilities will be a detriment to the society and those liabilities will be eliminated.

The collective society paradigm will be what must prevail. The individual is no longer a concern. The community, the society, is what must continue on, and all must contribute. If you do not contribute, you will be trained. If you are incapable of being trained or rehabilitated, you will be considered "in the eyes of the society" a liability. And liabilities are a hindrance to society and its sustainability. Thus, you will be dealt with accordingly, for the good of the society.

Then the Fundamental Transformation, prophesied by Bill Ayers and supported by thousands of Marxist elected officials and citizens, will begin: the New Republic of America; the United States Socialist Republic.

But this New America, this United States Socialist Republic must be firmly established before the new order can be put fully into place. Our form of government must be in a position where the USSR of new, is the leading contender for the top position in this new order. No Hillary or Obama or Biden will concede their powers to be a lesser player on the world stage.

This person who holds the position of the "Most Powerful in the World" is going to be holding such an incredible hand that they are going to be able to force their way into the Head of Household, so to speak. They, with all of America's resources, all her military prowess, all her manpower and technological innovations and wealth, will be able to define the term "Leader of the Free World" as it has never been defined before.

The problem is that there is only one way to get America and Americans to accept this reconstruction, this Fundamental Transformation. Dissent and division, on a massive scale. And I wrote this book because the beginnings of this dissent are what we are witnessing today.

The Liberal/Marxist Machine must sow as much dissent and division among the people as possible. Divide and conquer was the tactic employed by Bill Ayers. Get the masses so disgusted with those in power that a new political elite is installed. A progressive political Machine that begins an unprecedented political/socio-economic move of unparalleled magnitude, on the heels of a seismic crisis. The Machine will take action to secure its rightful position, to rectify the problem, and then begin to eliminate the people's rights and control over their own destiny. The Machine will eliminate America's borders and allow millions of migrant immigrants seeking asylum to flood the country. The Machine will abolish the rule of law. It will incarcerate any who go against the grain or refuse to provide services and goods to all, regardless of compensation.

Then the folks with consolidated power can begin to unravel the system, appear to be genuinely concerned for the population, and deliver a solution that only they can see as practical. They will begin to institute a solution of fairness and equality, and present the masses a paradigm of justice for all, and power to the people. The people of the world will be encouraged to unite, ushering in their new era of common prosperity, but devoid of true free market capitalism.

"We all are part of the human race," will be the cadence. And the new society will bring peace and sustainability to the planet, where all who contribute will reap the benefits—an entire world community, working together to bring peace and obliterate hunger and poverty...**AND THE LIBERAL-MINDED MASSES WILL BUY IT HOOK, LINE AND SINKER.**

However, the protagonists will leave out one very important element in this equation.

"All who Contribute" will mean something else entirely. The masses will only hear the intention, not the reality. The reality will be so catastrophic to the psyche of the people that, once revealed, it will simply shock the people into compliance. Citizens will realize that resistance is futile, and cooperation is beneficial.

This ideal that the Liberal/Marxist Machine envisions for the world government is right around the corner; peeking out like a child trying to hide, but who gives themselves away by giggling. It will be launched (if we allow it) right here in America, as the rest of the world's nations follow. Just for a moment, reflect on where much of the chaos and outrage that has fueled this false narrative and perception of injustice, inequality, and awful disparity have come from. The Liberal/Marxist Machine right here in America, with the help of Karl Marx and our good buddy William Charles Ayers.

Marx's solution was "only one Class of people." The working class. He felt that man's greatest resource was his labor. And whoever controls that resource will truly be the wealthiest most powerful person on earth. Robert Muller is reported to have said, "We Must have a One World Government and a One World Leader as quickly as possible." Ayers and the Machine want revolution to build this utopia, and, should the Liberal/Marxist Machine get control of the three branches of our government, the duly elected "Most Powerful person in the World" will surely sell America out.

As Dr. Sowell so eloquently explains, these disparities, these adverse impacts for some, are the result of the natural human condition. Their exaggeration fuels the division and perpetuates the narrative so clearly that people of average intelligence are convinced that action on their part will bring about solutions, or "change." Antifa is a perfect example of the fear that is perpetuated by the Machine. Notice now, that Antifa is committing political warfare on America and Americans with mayhem and destruction of property. They claim that their mission is to keep America from turning into a fascist dictatorship . . . and they are using fascist tactics to do this. Rarely has the world seen such ignorance coming from intelligent adults. The only good thing is that they really do not pose a serious threat to America and her national security…yet. They are little more than local thugs with financing and can be dealt with if they become a real problem. Believe me when I tell you, their days of destruction are short-lived. As you are reading about this, I'm confident their leaders are being flagged and tagged by our local law enforcement and Department of Homeland Security.

In America, the powers that be let these "conditions" run as they might, and then once the smoke has cleared, our judicial system will remove the detritus. America will be back to business as usual. But, today, that seems a distant vision.

Dr. Sowell points out the reality of many of the disparities, and he knows full well the outcomes and the advantages and the disadvantages of living in a free society. Here he explains, in plain, familiar language, how these things take place. No embellishments. Simple, honest, straightforward unvarnished truth.

This is the mark of a reality-based true intellectual with a firm understanding of our social world and the human condition. It is so refreshing to read these words and hear them as they are true and decent, rather than poisoned by hate, and pride and vanity. Sowell clearly articulates how discrimination will always be with us and how cultures adapt.

Racial Discrimination is usually not very discriminating in the sense in which a wine connoisseur is discriminating in being able to detect subtle differences in tastes, aromas, or vintages. When Marian Anderson was refused permission to sing in Washington's Constitution Hall in 1939, it had nothing to do with her characteristics as a singer or as a person. She was black and that was it. Similarly in baseball, before Jackie Robinson broke the color line in 1947, no one cared what kind or quality of pitcher Satchel Paige was or how powerful a slugger Josh Gibson was. They were black and that was enough to keep them out.

If we are to examine discrimination and its consequences today, we cannot be as indiscriminate as the racists of the past or present. We must make distinctions—first as to some consistent meaning of the word "discrimination" and then in deriving criteria for determining when it applies. We must also distinguish discrimination from other social or cultural factors that produce economic and other differences in outcome for different individuals and groups.

Meanings of Discrimination

To many—perhaps most—Americans, there is racial discrimination when different rules and standards are applied to people who differ by race. To these Americans, there is "a level playing field" when the same rules and the same standards apply to everybody, regardless of race.

As traditional as this meaning of discrimination has been, a radically different conception of discrimination has a strong hold on many in the media and the academic world today as well as among political and legal elites. For them, differences in "life chances" define discrimination. If a black child does not have the same likelihood as a white child of growing up to become an executive or a scientist, then there is racial discrimination by this definition, even if the same rules and standards are applied to both in schools, the workplace, and everywhere else.

For those with this definition of discrimination, creating "a level playing field" means equalizing probabilities of success. Criteria which operate to prevent this are considered by them to be discriminatory in effect, even if not in intent.

Whatever definition—accompanying set of policies—one believes in, a serious discussion of racial discrimination or of racial issues in general requires that we lay our cards face up on the table and not hide behind ambiguous and shifting words that render any attempt at dialog futile and ultimately poisonous.

For purposes of our discussion here, the definition of "discrimination" will be the traditional one. Other views behind other definitions will not be dismissed, however, but will in fact be examined closely.

Cause and Effect

Definitions are not chosen out of thin air. Underlying different definitions of racial discrimination are different beliefs about the way the world operates. So long as these beliefs confront each other only as opposing dogmas, there is no resolution other than by trying to shout each other down or prevail by force, whether political or physical.

Many people believe that differences in life chances or differences in socioeconomic results are unusual, suspicious, and probably indicative of biased or malign social processes that operate to the detriment of particular racial and other groups.

While there have certainly been numerous examples of discrimination—in the traditional sense of applying different rules or standards to different groups—in the United States and in other countries around the world, that is very different from claiming the converse, that group differences in prospects or outcomes must derive from this source.

Intergroup differences have been the rule, not the exception, in countries around the world and throughout centuries of history.

Today, one need only turn on a television set and watch a professional basketball game to see that the races are not evenly or randomly represented in this sport and are not in proportion to their representation in the general population of the United States. Racially, the teams do not "look like America."

Although not visible to the naked eye, neither do the beer companies that sponsor this and other athletic events. Most, if not all, of the leading beer-producing companies in the United States were founded by people of German ancestry. So were most of the leading piano manufacturers.

Nor is German domination of these two industries limited to the United States.

The kind of demographic over-representation in particular lines of work found among blacks in basketball or Germans in beer brewing and piano-making can also be found among Jews in the apparel industry—not just in contemporary New York but also in the history of medieval Spain, the Ottoman Empire, the Russian Empire, Brazil, Germany, and Chile. At one time, most of the clothing stores in Melbourne were owned by Jews, who have never been as much as one percent of the Australian population.

Most of the people laying cable in Sydney, Australia, are of Irish ancestry. All the billionaires in Thailand and Indonesia are of Chinese ancestry. Four-fifths of the doughnut shops in California are owned by people of Cambodian ancestry. The list goes on and on.

It would be no feat to fill a book with statistical disparities that have nothing to do with discrimination.1 What would be a real feat would be to get people to realize that correlation is not causation---especially when the numbers fit their preconceptions.

Very often the group predominating in a particular field has no power to keep others out, except by excelling in the particular activity. Blacks cannot discriminate against whites in basketball, where the franchises are owned by whites. The Chinese minority in Malaysia or Indonesia cannot stop Malaysians or Indonesians from opening businesses, though historically most of the major domestic enterprises in both countries were created by people of

Chinese ancestry. Nor could immigrants from India stop either blacks or whites from opening businesses in Kenya, though Indian entrepreneurs were once so predominant in Kenya and other parts of East Africa that the rupee became the predominant currency in that region.

Some statistical disparities are of course caused by discrimination, just as some deaths are caused by cancer. But one cannot infer discrimination from statistics any more than one can infer cancer whenever someone dies. The absence of corroborating evidence of discrimination has forced some into claiming that the discrimination has been so "subtle," "covert," or "unconscious" as to leave no tangible evidence. But this method of arguing—where both the presence and the absence of empirical evidence prove the same thing—would prove anything about anything anywhere and anytime.

Lastly, we are seeing a rapid decline in support for our police and sheriffs in America, that is coming off of the recent deaths relating to intense physical altercations with police.

Rather than go into the Who, What and Whys of police issues, suffice it to say that the false narratives that the police are racists is being perversely perpetuated around the nation, and are fueling the protests we are seeing. These lies are tearing America apart. These lies are fueling the hatred. In retaliation, the radical liberal protesters, cheered on by the Liberal/Marxists, burn down and destroy their own neighborhoods.

And burning down your own neighborhood NEVER does any community any good.

These protesters' numbers amount to barely 1/10th of one percent of the U.S. population. These groups do not pose a serious threat to national security as they are local and limited. What keeps me up at night is the reality that there are hundreds of Marxist elected officials already in our government today, with the power to guide our government into ruinous socialist shores.

The mainstream media and news outlets covering these protests are taking an active role in distorting the reality, exaggerating the narrative of social unrest. They are frequently spinning the facts to fit the Marxist narrative, and are therefore complicit. Most adults in America understand this discrepancy. Children cannot.

6

The Means: Blackmail

NO JUSTICE, NO PEACE

The American people are being blackmailed. And things will not get any better any time soon. Let me pull back the curtain, in case you haven't already noticed. Regrettably, we are seeing an increase in Socialist politicians being elected or appointed to powerful positions in local and federal government. These people are right in among us, advancing the Liberal/Marxist world view, while we conservatives, both young and old, seem to accept their folly as merely rhetoric.

IT IS NOT RHETORIC; IT IS A HARSH AND EVER-PRESENT REALITY

Let's start with the person that orchestrated, managed and facilitated the Capital Hill Autonomous Zone (CHAZ) Protest that took over City Hall and a six square-block area of downtown Seattle in June of 2020: Kshawa Sawant, Seattle City Councilwoman.

Sawant opened the city hall doors and let the protesters in and helped in orchestrating the Occupy City Hall group and its members to take over the 6-block area of downtown Seattle as an Autonomous Zone.

Ms. Sawant is a Socialist; A card-carrying member of SAP the Socialist Alternative Party.

Ms. Sawant has an associate. Congresswoman Pramila Jayapal. Jayapal is the Co-Chairman of the Congressional Progressive Caucus. This Liberal

Left-leaning Caucus is not simply liberal. It is overtly Marxist. As it claims to be a Liberal progressive caucus that leans left – far left—it is a major cog in the Liberal/Marxist Machine.

This is a venue for intensely "Progressive/Socialist" Democrats, who hide under the liberal banner pretending to be patriots. But make no mistake, they are not patriots in the vernacular of traditional American rights and freedoms. These folks are Marxists. Their agenda, clearly stated, is "Fundamental Social Transformation" of our government and society. They cry out "meaningful social reforms." Sorry folks. Let's call them what they are. They are Marxists. Many of the 97 members of the Congressional Progressive Caucus are devout members of the DSA: the Democratic Socialists of America. As such, they are in an acute way very close relatives of the Socialist Alternative Party of America.

Take a look at the fifty Marxists in Congress today:

2019 LIST OF SOCIALISTS AND COMMUNISTS IN CONGRESS
Trevor Loudon

A friend of mine was challenged to name "even two socialists in Congress." Altogether, if you add in Islamist connections, I think about 100 members of the House of Representatives would struggle to pass a low-level background security check, but guess what? There are no security checks in Congress.

Here's my list of 50 of the most obvious socialists in the House, with links to my website for the backup evidence. Apologies to the many I've omitted. Please email me at trevor.newzeal@gmail.com if you'd like to be included in future lists.

Raul Grijalva (D AZ) has worked closely with the Communist Party USA since at least 1993. A self-described "Alinskyite." Traveled to Cuba in 2015.

Ami Bera (D CA) Has used Communist Party USA campaign for volunteers in 2010, 2014 and 2016. Also close to Democratic Socialists of America.

Nancy Pelosi (D CA) Very close to several key Communist Party USA allies in San Francisco in the 1970s and '80s. Also some involvement with Democratic Socialists of America.

Barbara Lee (D CA) Lee has been close to the Communist Party USA for decades. In the 1990s she was a leading member of the Communist Party spin-off Committees of Correspondence. Has been to Cuba more than 20 times.

Ro Khanna (D CA) Very close to Democratic Socialists of America.

Salud Carbajal (D CA) Long history with Democratic Socialists of America members.

Judy Chu (D CA) Was heavily involved with the now defunct pro-Beijing Communist Workers Party in the 1970s and '80s. Still works closely with former members today. China's best friend in the US Congress.

Raul Ruiz (D CA) Worked closely with Workers World Party members in Massachusetts in the late 1990s.

Karen Bass (D CA) Was actively involved with the Marxist-Leninist group. Line of March in the 1980s. Still works closely with former members. Mentored by a leading Communist Party USA member. Also close to Democratic Socialists of America and some Freedom Road Socialist Organization members. Has been to Cuba at least 4 times.

Maxine Waters (D CA) Long history with the Communist Party USA. Also ties to some Communist Workers Party and Workers World Party fronts. Has employed staff members from Democratic Socialists of America and League of Revolutionary Struggle.

Joe Courtney (D CT) Has worked closely with several Communist Party USA leaders.

Rosa DeLauro (D CT) Has worked extremely closely with the Communist Party USA for many years. Traveled to Cuba in 2014.

Jim Himes (D CT) His 1988 thesis "The Sandinista Defense Committees and the Transformation of Political Culture in Nicaragua" was a sympathetic portrayal of Marxist government's civilian spy network. Has worked closely with one Communist Party USA front group.

Kathy Castor (D FL) Has worked closely with Cuba and pro-Castro organizations to open US trade with the communist island.

John Lewis (D GA) Worked closely with the Communist Party USA and Socialist Party USA in the 1960s. In recent years has worked with Democratic Socialists of America members.

Tulsi Gabbard (D HI) Has worked with Democratic Socialists of America members through her political career. Ties to some Filipino-American "former communists." Worked with Communist Party USA–affiliated former Congressman Dennis Kucinich to defend Soviet-Russian puppet Syrian leader Bashar-al-Assad.

Bobby Rush (D IL) Former leader of the Maoist-leaning Black Panther Party. Has worked closely with Communist Party USA and Democratic Socialists of America. Has traveled to Cuba twice.

Jesus "Chuy" Garcia (D IL) Has worked closely with the Communist Party USA for nearly 40 years.

Danny Davis (D IL) Was a member of Democratic Socialists of America in the mid 2000s. Has worked closely with the Communist Party USA since the 1980s. Also close to Committees of Correspondence in the 1990s.

Jan Schakowsky (D IL) Was a member of Democratic Socialists of America in the 1980s and has continued to work closely with the organization. Has also worked closely with some Communist Party USA members.

Dave Loebsack (D IA) Has worked closely with Socialist Party USA and Democratic Socialists of America members for many years.

John Yarmuth (D KY) has worked with Committees of Correspondence for Democracy and Socialism members. Traveled to Cuba in 2011.

Jamie Raskin (D MD) Has worked closely with Democratic Socialists of America for many years.

Jim McGovern (D MA) has supported Latin American socialist and revolutionary groups for 20 years Has traveled to Cuba at least three times.

Ayanna Pressley (D MA) Has been endorsed by Democratic Socialists of America. Worked with Freedom Road Socialist Organization front groups and with the pro-Beijing Chinese Progressive Association in Boston.

Andy Levin (D MI) Close to Democratic Socialists of America for at least a decade.

Rashida Talib (D MI) Democratic Socialists of America member.

Betty McCollum (D MN) Close ties to communist Laos. Has worked with Democratic Socialists of America members. Traveled to Cuba in 2014.

Ilhan Omar (D MN) Supported by Democratic Socialists of America controlled groups. Our Revolution and National Nurses United. Reportedly a self-described "democratic socialist."

Bennie Thompson (D MS) Was close to the Communist Party USA for many years. Also supported the Communist Workers Party organization. Traveled to Cuba in 2000 and worked with Fidel Castro to train leftist American medical students in Cuba.

William Lacy Clay (D MO) Has worked with Communist Party USA fronts for many years.

Greg Meeks (D NY) Has traveled to Cuba at least 3 times. Was a strong supporter of Venezuelan dictator Hugo Chavez.

Grace Meng (D NY) Very close to the pro-Beijing Asian Americans for Equality. Was also active in a radical Korean-American organization.

Nydia Velasquez (D NY) Close ties to Democratic Socialists of America. Welcomed Fidel Castro to Harlem in 1995.

Yvette Clarke (D NY) Addressed a Workers World Party rally in 2005. Close ally of a prominent Democratic Socialists of America member. Traveled to Cuba in 2007.

Jerry Nadler (D NY) Was a member of Democratic Socialist Organizing Committee in the 1970s and was involved with Democratic Socialists of America in the 1980s and 1990s.

Alexandria Ocasio-Cortez (D NY) Member of Democratic Socialists of America.

Jose Serrano (D NY) Close ties to the Communist Party USA and Democratic Socialists of America. Was a strong supporter of Venezuelan dictator Hugo Chavez.

G. K. Butterfield (D NC) Some connection to Workers World Party and Freedom Road Socialist Organization. Also close to the "former" communist-led Moral Mondays movement.

Marcy Kaptur (D OH) Ties to Democratic Socialists of America. Traveled to Cuba in 2002.

Earl Blumenauer (D OR) Ties to Democratic Socialists of America.

Steve Cohen (D TN) Close ties to Memphis Socialist Party USA members. Traveled to Cuba in 2011.

Sylvia Garcia (D TX) Elected to the Texas state house with Communist Party USA support. Works closely with a major communist-influenced organization.

Eddie Bernice Johnson (D TX) Long relationship with the Communist Party USA. Traveled to Cuba at least twice.

Marc Veasy (D TX) Very close relationship with the Communist Party USA.

Lloyd Doggett (D TX) Has been involved with Democratic Socialists of America since the 1980s.

Pramila Jayapal (D WA) Has been involved with Freedom Road Socialist Organization connected groups for many years.

Mark Pocan (D WI) Close to some Democratic Socialists of America activists. Long-time active supporter of Colombian revolutionary movements.

Gwen Moore (D WI) Has been mentored by leading Democratic Socialists of America and Communist Party USA members.

Eleanor Holmes North (D DC) Former Young People's Socialist League member. Long connection to Democratic Socialists of America.

These particular elected officials are just a part of the Liberal/Marxist Machine within our government. There is one particular person I would like to point out, who is no longer a Congressmember, but is the Attorney General for the State of Minnesota. His name is Keith Ellison.

Interestingly, then Congressman Keith Ellison of MN has actually endorsed Antifa. He tweeted an endorsement while holding a copy of the antifa handbook. This guy is right in here among us. A sitting U.S. Representative showing support on social media for a group that is clearly aligned with the radical violent left, and the Marxist agenda.

KEITH ELLISON ENDORSES POLITICAL VIOLENCE
On January 04, 2018

Shockingly, Minnesota Congressman Keith Ellison, deputy chairman of the Democratic National Committee, has come out in favor of political violence. Yesterday he tweeted an endorsement of the fascist Antifa group, which has rioted in cities across the country. Antifa members wear masks and wield baseball bats and ax handles, attacking innocent bystanders, smashing store windows, burning vehicles, and otherwise engaging in political violence. Yesterday Ellison tweeted this photo of himself with Antifa's manifesto.

Now let's shift gears. The Socialist Alternative Party here in America has for many years professed socio-economic transformation, and now has an ally in the Black Lives Matter movement. Here is an excerpt from their website, endorsing the BLM organization.

Black Lives Matter and Marxism 6/16/20 Taken from document drafted by Eljeer Hawkins and approved by Socialist Alternative's National Committee, February 2015

We have entered a new phase in the struggle against racism and capitalism in the United States. "Black Lives Matter" (BLM) started after the death of Trayvon Martin and then became a protest movement. The BLM banner is a powerful affirmation of the humanity of black workers, poor and youth. Every 28 hours a black or brown person is killed by police, vigilante or extra-judicial violence. Police kill black Americans at nearly the same rate as the lynchings during the Jim Crow era; young black men are 21 times more likely to be shot dead by police than white men. BLM has captured the imagination of a generation of new activists in the U.S. and globally.

This is a reemergence of the black masses onto the scene of U.S. history after decades of defeat, sell-outs, decimation and mass incarceration. The current radicalization must be seen in the context of the limits given by the immediate past of a low-level of general class consciousness in society and a historically very low level of struggle in the black community. This is further complicated by the lack of militancy of the remaining civil rights leadership from the 1960s and '70s; those who weren't assassinated or imprisoned have largely been bought off and co-opted by the establishment. The Obama Presidency both signifies the limits of pro-capitalist identity politics and also gives confidence to black youth that they could get support in society and can defeat racism.

The revolt against police violence took new form in Ferguson and New York in recent months, with daily determined demonstrations and a new layer of activists emerging. There is partial rejection of the old civil rights leadership, which is uneven geographically and generationally, and new organizations thrown up by struggle.

The mood to fight is influenced by the economic crisis and Occupy. At its height, the protests took mass direct action to block highways and occupy symbols of police violence, economic inequality and racism. Now, the movement is in at least partial retreat. There is a danger that the advanced activists will cut themselves off from the broader masses by taking isolated direct action. We should advocate tactics and a strategy that give the activists an approach that can bring broader layers along with them.

The first phase of the movement is over, but the new activists aren't going away, and a new phase will emerge. This has been only one wave of struggle. There will be more atrocities, more protests, more movements in the coming months and years.

Socialists, while building actions to indict the killer cops and win demands against racist policing, also need to boldly connect the dots to a program that can defeat racism in all its forms. We must connect the battle against police violence to clear economic demands: for a $15 an hour minimum wage and massive jobs programs as well as quality education and housing. We must put forward tactics of mass action while calling on unions and organizations like the NAACP – where they have influence – to support this struggle. We put forward our slogans and demands to be taken up by the broader movement because we want to point towards victories in the here and now. But we must also boldly point to a socialist solution and the need to build a multiracial socialist force in the fight to once and for all end poverty, racism and corporate domination.[30]

These previous paragraphs denote the socialist agenda of which I speak. Now, please take close note of how the article's final paragraph, describing how the socialist leaders see themselves as shaping a movement involving hundreds of thousands of Americans across the country to take action.

The BLM movement opens a new powerful chapter. The previous radical black freedom movement always had powerful anti-capitalist, socialist, and internationalist currents. Today black and Latino youth are increasingly open to the ideas of socialism and Marxism. Let's engage this movement with confidence, armed with our ideas and the lessons of history. The struggle of the multiracial working class for socialist change is the beginning of overcoming racial division. Overthrowing capitalism cannot end all aspects of racism overnight, but it can do away with the exploitation that lays the basis for class society's divide-and-rule approach. There is no other road. Black liberation can only be won through the socialist transformation of society.

Now let's shift gears again, focusing on public officials who align themselves with the Marxist dialectic. These elected officials, local, statewide and federal; communicate among themselves frequently. They do not hold town hall meetings. They do not hold public sit-down conversations. They convene in private thru text, e-mails, (privately) and through social media.

---

30 https://www.socialistalternative.org/marxism-fight-black-freedom/black-lives-matter-marxism/

Many of these protests we see must be orchestrated, financed and managed. George Soros's Open Society has over 300 far-left radical organizations, affiliates here in America, working the 501{c} 3 non-profit and social justice gambit. These affiliates provide funding and people for many of these riots. The Ferguson riots were full of folks from all over the country. They were hired through social media., by these affiliates of the Open Society…and promised upwards of $2,000.00 for their efforts as well as travel to and from.

If you would like to look into these Open Society affiliates and educate yourself, I encourage you to start with "Discover the Networks" website by David Horowitz. If you follow the links and spend the time to search out and educate yourself about all these organizations and how they are tied together, you will see that they communicate through government interactions and meetings and Board rooms. They network, then spread out the information to their followers through social media. Networking and management and orchestration on a national level…THE MEANS

And here is the part that really concerns me. These organizers and organizations are aligning with Islamic organizations here in our country. Make No Mistake many of these Islamic organizations hide under the banner of peaceful Muslims. Ladies and gentlemen, roughly eighty percent are strict followers of the Islamic Faith. Civilizational Jihad is the undercurrent, and Sharia Law is the defining code of conduct. Please look for the Steven Emerson documentary "Jihad in America: The Grand Deception"

The Six Phase goal of Islamic Jihad is to "Change the Constitution of America". According to Emerson, we are now in the Sixth Phase of the Islamic Jihadist movement, which is Total Confrontation. You will find deep-rooted information in the website "Unconstrained Analytics" about the Islamic ties to these protests, protestors and organizations, authored by Major Stephen Coughlin (ret.). Coughlin is a former intelligence analyst for the Department of Defense, and the author of "Catastrophic Failure", the eye-opening book at how we missed the signs of 9/11.

The last word, and the final results.

All my life I have tried to be pragmatic, and look for solutions.

As probably the most pragmatic guy we've seen in decades, Trump has put some rather serious issues in America on notice. One such issue is the Common Core State Standards {Curriculum} that Obama slipped in and coerced States to adopt mentioned it earlier}

Much of what we have seen happening, as I have tried to point out, is the result of the coordinated assault on our elementary school age children by Socialist / Marxist teachers, educators, administrators and Marxist elected officials.

Over a thirty-year period, our youngest most precious loves have been under an assault. The results of the handiwork of these Neo-Marxists, we are now witnessing in cities and towns across America. This collective disregard for American Exceptionalism and complete disregard for parental and judicial authority, is fueling the riots and protests we see being played out on every channel and media across the globe. And the calamity and destruction, just seems to never end. But it Will. Of that I am confident. There are millions of good, honest hardworking Patriots in America, that will not let this country be torn down, then re-shaped into some misguided Liberal / Marxist Ideal. Of that I am extremely confident.

But Americans who truly love America the way it is…must get involved. Just your Vote will not be enough. Talk with your children. Pay attention to the school curriculum, and how it effect's your child's homework, school work, attitudes and behavior.

President Trump has taken steps to bring education home, where it belongs, to the states and local school boards. And, in addition, he seeks to engage those most important in the decision-making process that effects a child's life; **Parents**. He wants to limit the controls that Obama's nationalized Education program has used for the past twenty years to mold American minds. This is where we begin to take back our country

President Trump Proposes Transformative, Student-First Budget to Return Power to States, Limit Federal Control of Education

Budget Calls for Expanding Education Freedom, Block Granting K-12 Education Funds, and a Separate and Reformed Federal Student Aid

Adds New Funding to Support Children with Disabilities, Career and Technical Education for All Students

FEBRUARY 10, 2020

WASHINGTON — The President released today his budget request for the U.S. Department of Education for the 2021 fiscal year. This transformative, student-first budget prioritizes improving student achievement, reducing the outsized Federal role in education, and returning control over education decisions to whom it belongs—State and local leaders, teachers, parents, and students.

The budget calls for consolidating nearly all existing K-12 formula and competitive grant programs into one block grant to States, called the Elementary and Secondary Education for the Disadvantaged (ESED) Block Grant. Funds would be allocated using the same formulas as the Title I Grants to Local Educational Agencies program. The budget also builds on the multi-year Federal Student Aid (FSA) reform project U.S. Education Secretary Betsy DeVos launched in 2018 to improve management, oversight, and administration of student aid programs. To that end, the budget also proposes to answer a question Secretary DeVos asked at last year's FSA training conference: Why isn't FSA a stand-alone government corporation, run by a professional, expert, and apolitical Board of Governors?

"This budget proposal is about one thing—putting students and their needs above all else," said Secretary DeVos. "That starts with creating Education Freedom Scholarships and helping 1 million more students find the best educational fit for them. We know education freedom helps students succeed, and it's long past time for Congress to act to give students and their families more choices and more control.

"Our budget puts an end to education earmarks. Instead of Washington politicians and bureaucrats forcing local schools to spend limited resources on D.C.'s priorities, this budget proposes putting state and local leaders, teachers, parents, and students themselves in control of education. Our block grant proposal simply aligns the resources with the law of the land—the Every Student Succeeds Act. States will be free to focus on people, not paperwork. Results, not regulations. We know States will spend their money differently, and that's okay. In fact, that's what we hope they do. They know best how to serve their students.

"We also propose making critical new investments in supporting children with disabilities, moving closer to fulfilling Congress' promise to fully fund the Individuals with Disabilities Education Act (IDEA). And we're asking for new resources for career and technical education to ensure every student in America has access to skills training to help them prepare for successful careers.

"Our proposal further asks Congress to partner with us in studying the Office of Federal Student Aid becoming a stand-alone entity. FSA has, in recent years, essentially ballooned into a $1.5 trillion bank that has outgrown its current governance structure. Students and their families deserve better from FSA. In the meantime, we're continuing to build on our important customer-centric Next Generation reforms. Through a singular FSA platform, operating system, and unified website, we will provide customers with a seamless student loan experience from application through repayment. We're also providing students with more information than ever before so they can make better decisions about how they finance their education."

Highlights from the President's FY 2021 Budget Request include the following:

Expanding Education Freedom for Students

Education Freedom Scholarships (EFS) would provide up to $5 billion in additional education funding to help more than 1 million students across the country find their education fit

This proposal would dramatically expand the options available to families

States, not the Federal government, will design their own programs aimed at serving their students. Each State's family eligibility requirements and allowable uses of scholarship funds will be aligned with their State's unique needs

Funded by private, voluntary donations, EFS does not do a thing to change any funding amount already allocated to public school students or public school teachers

Empowering States to Best Meet the Needs of Students

The Elementary and Secondary Education for the Disadvantaged (ESED) Block Grant consolidates most

K-12 formula and competitive grant programs administered by the Department into one $19.4 billion formula grant program

This proposal builds on the promise of ESSA and right-sizes the Federal role in education by empowering States and school districts to spend Federal taxpayer funds the way they see fit to best support their most disadvantaged students

Funds would be allocated using the same formulas as the Title I Grants to Local Educational Agencies program

States and local districts could use the funds for any authorized purposes of the consolidated programs, while continuing to meet accountability and reporting requirements aimed at protecting students, supporting school improvement, and providing parents the information they need to make education decisions for their children

Increasing Career and Technical Education Opportunities for Students

The FY 2021 budget request dramatically increases funding for Career and Technical Education (CTE) programs by $900 million

This supports the Administration's goal of ensuring every high school student in America has access to CTE programs that provide multiple, high-quality pathways to success after graduation

This request includes $2 billion, an increase of $680 million, for CTE State Grants to support high-quality CTE programs in high school and postsecondary institutions and $90 million, an increase of $83 million, for CTE National Programs to support high-quality CTE programs in STEM, including computer science

The budget also renews the President's proposal to double the American Competitiveness and Workforce Improvement Act fee for the H-1B visa program which could generate an estimated $117 million in additional funding for the CTE State Grants program

Transforming Federal Student Aid to Better Serve Students

This budget request proposes continued modernization of all aspects of FSA in order to better serve its customers, including a call for an evaluation of FSA as a separate organization, with reformed governance

A new governance model would lead to improved management, oversight, and administration of student aid programs

The budget also proposes to simplify the Federal student loan programs and student loan repayment by reducing the numerous and complicated loan types, establishing reasonable annual and lifetime limits on those loans, providing higher education institutions more flexibility to help students avoid overborrowing, and streamlining income-based repayment plans

The budget request continues to fund the multi-year Next Generation (Next Gen) student aid platform improvements, including the development and implementation of a new mobile-first, singular loan servicing platform that consolidates all customer-facing websites into one and provides customers with a seamless experience from application through repayment.

Conclusion

It seems that the Liberal/Marxist Machine here in America has convinced many of their devoted followers that it is only through dissent, division and destruction, followed by collective transformation of America, will our country become what it should be; free from all injustice, racism and inequality.

I for one really do not want to live in THAT country.

That country will shear its sheep once a year; and dispose of them just as quickly. In other words, the individual concerns, hopes and dreams of Americans will no longer be of any consequence.

It appears that many folks that call themselves Liberals and want this transformation to take place, actually hate America with all of its freedoms; despite the fact that America has lifted man out of darkness in many ways, and improved his quality of life to the point where every individual, can choose their own path, mark their own way, Choose their own Destiny..

If these so-called democrats that long for a "Fundamentally Transformed America" call themselves Americans, then I am ashamed to call myself one.

The Machine in America has absolutely no desire to follow the Rule of Law. It will stop at nothing to achieve its goal. It is following the Alinsky model that "the Ends justify the Means". As Senator Lindsey Graham observed, this indeed puts democracy in danger.

Democracy is the foundation for our freedoms, and Marxism is a clearly visible threat.

Democracy has its roots in the Rule of Law, and it is our single most important safeguard against tyranny. America's forefathers fled tyranny in Europe, and established a country like no other in the history of humanity. America has made the world a better place for mankind. That's why millions of people have crossed deserts and oceans to get here. And today, they and our children are being told lies; that America isn't truly great, that it is rife with poverty and racism. And yet, they still come.

It begs the Question "Ever Wonder Why?"

I want to share with you the most profound and practical answer to this question anyone can ask of themselves or the world, "ever wonder why?" Dr. Thomas Sowell answers this question in the most simple and direct terms.

Ever Wonder Why? Thomas Sowell

When you have seen scenes of poverty and squalor in many Third World countries, either in person or in pictures, have you ever wondered why we in America have been spared such a fate? When you have learned of the bitter oppressions that so many people have suffered under, in despotic countries around the world, have you ever wondered why Americans have been spared? Have scenes of government-sponsored carnage and lethal mob violence in countries like Rwanda or in the Balkans ever made you wonder why such horrifying scenes are not found on the streets of America? Nothing is easier than to take for granted what we are used to, and to imagine that it is more or less natural, so that it requires no explanation. Instead, many Americans demand explanations of why things are not even better and express indignation that they are not. Some people think the issue is whether the glass is half empty or half full. More fundamentally, the question is whether the glass started out empty or started out full.

U.nited S.tates S.ocialist R.epublic™

Those who are constantly looking for the "root causes" of poverty, of crime, and of other national and international problems, act as if prosperity and law-abiding behavior were so natural that it is their absence which has to be explained. But a casual glance around the world today, or back through history, would dispel any notion that good things just happen naturally, much less inevitably. 4 ever wonder why? The United States of America is the exception, not the rule. Once we realize that America is an exception, we might even have a sense of gratitude for having been born here, even if gratitude has become un-cool in many quarters. At the very least, we might develop some concern for seeing that whatever has made this country better off is not lost or discarded—or eroded away, bit by bit, until it is gone. Those among us who are constantly rhapsodizing about "change" in vague and general terms seem to have no fear that a blank check for change can be a huge risk in a world where so many other countries that are different are also far worse off. Chirping about "change" may produce a giddy sense of excitement or of personal exaltation but, as usual, the devil is in the details. Even despotic countries that have embraced sweeping changes have often found that these were changes for the worse. The czars in Russia, the shah of Iran, the Batista regime in Cuba, were all despotic. But they look like sweethearts compared to the regimes that followed. For example, the czars never executed as many people in half a century as Stalin did in one day. Even the best countries must make changes and the United States has made many economic, social, and political changes for the better. But that is wholly different from making "change" a mantra. To be for or against "change" in general is childish. Everything depends on the specifics. To be for generic "change" is to say that what we have is so bad that any change is likely to be for the better. Such a pose may make some people feel superior to others who find much that is worth preserving in our values, The Culture Wars 5 traditions and institutions. The status quo is never sacrosanct but its very existence proves that it is viable, as seductive theoretical alternatives may not turn out to be. Most Americans take our values, traditions and institutions so much for granted that they find it hard to realize how much all these things are under constant attack in our schools, our colleges, and in much of the press, the movies and literature. There is a culture war going on within the United States—and in fact, within Western civilization as a whole— which may ultimately have as much to do with our survival, or failure to survive, as the war on terrorism. There are all sorts of financial, ideological, and psychic rewards for undermining American society and its values. Unless some of us realize the existence of this culture war, and the high stakes in it, we can lose what cost those Americans before us so much to win and preserve.

Why do millions long to come here? Why do thousands of people come from all over the planet who were living in squalor and poverty, know that when they get here, their quality of life will improve a thousand-fold. It is because of what America is. It is a beacon in the darkness. They know what it stands for.

Yet, here in the greatest country on earth, we have people who intentionally want to tear America down. We have people who are so obsessed with its destruction, that they cannot see what the rest of the people here see, and are willing to fight and die for, to keep and protect.

When members of the Liberal / Marxist Machine in America, willingly violate the Rule of Law, and the Marxists, that sit on committee's in Congress and the Senate, violate their oath to uphold the Constitution, and actually fabricate tales about Supreme Court nominee's, then it may be time to take a breath and proclaim this cannot continue, and that these people must be held accountable for their lies.

Here, in the words of Dr. Thomas Sowell, is the most apt description of how the lies perpetuated by the Liberal/Marxist Machine can become a destructive power, and are truly the "money of fools."

The Money of Fools[31]

Seventeenth century philosopher Thomas Hobbes said that words are wise men's counters, but they are the money of fools.

That is as painfully true today as it was four centuries ago. Using words as vehicles to try to convey your meaning is very different from taking words so literally that the words use you and confuse you.

Take the simple phrase "rent control." If you take these words literally-- as if they were money in the bank-- you get a complete distortion of reality.

New York is the city with the oldest and strongest rent control laws in the nation. San Francisco is second. But if you look at cities with the highest average rents, New York is first and San Francisco is second. Obviously, "rent control" laws do not control rent.

If you check out the facts, instead of relying on words, you will discover that "gun control" laws do not control guns, the government's "stimulus" spending does not stimulate

---

31 RealClearPolitics. Sowell, T. *The Money of Fools*, © 2010, Creators Syndicate, Inc. https://www.realclearpolitics.com/articles/2010/09/14/the_money_of_fools_107138.html

the economy and that many "compassionate" policies inflict cruel results, such as the destruction of the black family.

Do you know how many millions of people died in the war "to make the world safe for democracy"-- a war that led to autocratic dynasties being replaced by totalitarian dictatorships that slaughtered far more of their own people than the dynasties had?

Warm, fuzzy words and phrases have an enormous advantage in politics. None has had such a long run of political success as "social justice."

The idea cannot be refuted because it has no specific meaning. Fighting it would be like trying to punch the fog. No wonder "social justice" has been such a political success for more than a century-- and counting.

While the term has no defined meaning, it has emotionally powerful connotations. There is a strong sense that it is simply not right-- that it is unjust-- that some people are so much better off than others.

Justification, even as the term is used in printing and carpentry, means aligning one thing with another. But what is the standard to which we think incomes or other benefits should be aligned?

Is the person who has spent years in school goofing off, acting up or fighting-- squandering the tens of thousands of dollars that the taxpayers have spent on his education-- supposed to end up with his income aligned with that of the person who spent those same years studying to acquire knowledge and skills that would later be valuable to himself and to society at large?

Some advocates of "social justice" would argue that what is fundamentally unjust is that one person is born into circumstances that make that person's chances in life radically different from the chances that others have-- through no fault of one and through no merit of the others.

Maybe the person who wasted educational opportunities and developed self-destructive behavior would have turned out differently if born into a different home or a different community.

That would of course be more just. But now we are no longer talking about "social" justice, unless we believe that it is all society's fault that different families and communities have different values and priorities-- and that society can "solve" that "problem."

Nor can poverty or poor education explain such differences. There are individuals who were raised by parents who were both poor and poorly educated, but who pushed their children to get the education that the parents themselves never had. Many individuals and groups would not be where they are today without that.

All kinds of chance encounters-- with particular people, information or circumstances-- have marked turning points in many individual's lives, whether toward fulfillment or ruin.

None of these things is equal or can be made equal. If this is an injustice, it is not a "social" injustice because it is beyond the power of society.

You can talk or act as if society is both omniscient and omnipotent. But, to do so would be to let words become what Thomas Hobbes called them, "the money of fools."

Ladies and Gentlemen, let me be specific. When these elected officials will fabricate out and out lies in order to achieve their agenda, then, as Congressman Devin Nunes puts it, "Our very lives are in danger." If we in America who call ourselves conservatives, and our conservative leadership do not take action, to hold accountable those Marxists who hide under the liberal banner and egregiously violate the rule of law in America, then we deserve whatever the Liberal / Marxist Machine forces upon us.

We must engage our fellow conservatives to protect what we have. Otherwise all that we love will be taken from us. We must righteously and legally use all our powers, our voice and our vote to fight this assault on our values, our lifestyle and our very lives.

We must convince the Liberal / Marxist Machine, these Neo-Marxists in America, that they can protest, riot, burn, pillage their own neighborhood—even destroy their own towns—and tear down every statue and offensive part of our history, but the Marxist Machine is, this day, put on notice. The people in this county who love America just the way it is, the moral majority, the patriots who have fought and died, the pioneers, trailblazers and industrialists of bygone years, and your God-fearing neighbor will never allow America to **"Be Fundamentally Transformed."**

Bibliography

Ayers, W., Fugitive Days: A Memoir. Autobiography. © Beacon Press, Boston. 2002 www.beacon.org

Ayers, W., Dohrn, B., *Prairie Fire: the Politics of Revolutionary Anti-Imperialsm*. Political Statement of the Weather Underground, May 1974 (reprint edition, PDF) From Students for a Democratic Society – SDS, Weatherman/Weather Underground Organization. 2020

Briggs, WM., *Prairie Fire in the Classroom: Bill Ayers's Bloodless Revolution*, (March 22, 2018) https://wmbriggs.com/post/24136/

Buckley, W., from *Firing Line* with William F. Buckley, Guest Saul Alinsky. Hoover Institution, Stanford University.1967 https://www.youtube.com/watch?v=M6ybDKaOlvg

Coulson, A. *Markets vs. Monopolies in Education: A Global Review of the Evidence*. Cato Institute, Center for Educational Freedom October 27, 2008. https://www.cato.org/publications/

Dorfman, J. *"Romney was wrong about the 47 percent, the problem is much worse."* Forbes magazine, December 19, 2013. www.forbes.com

Dyson, EM. *Tears We Cannot Stop: A Sermon to White America.* © St. Martin's Press. 2017. ISBN: 9781250135995

Joffe, M., and Ring, E. *California's State and Local Liabilities Total $1.5 Trillion*, California Policy Center, January 3, 2019. www.californiapolicycenter.org

McCluskey, N., *Getting the Common Core (and Federal) Facts Right.* 2016. https://www.cato.org/

Miller, P. *Willfully Ignorant.* fiction. © WestBow Press, 2014.

Muller, R. *Appeal to All Leaders of Nations.* Ideas and Dreams for a Better World, September 2000. www.RobertMuller.com

Munk, The Debates- "Political Correctness"; Toronto, Ontario, CA. May 18, 2018. https://www.youtube.com/watch?v=MNjYSns0op0

Naimark, N. *"Stalin's Genocides".* © Princeton University Press. 2011

Nordlinger, J. *"Guilty as Sin. Free as a Bird"* National Review. August 28, 2008. www.nationalreview.com

Reid, IA, *Building the Machine: An investigative documentary into the Common Core State Standards Initiative*, produced by Home School Legal Defense Association, 2014.

Rosenberg, S., Weather Underground and Thousand Currents, Capital Research Center, InfluenceWatch, 2020. www.influencewatch.org

Sowell, T. *"Black rednecks and white liberals".* © Encounter books, San Francisco. 2005

Sowell, T. "The Money of Fools", © Creators Syndicate, Inc. 2010

Thiessen, M., *Thanks to Jonathan Gruber for revealing Obamacare deception.* The Washington Post, November 17, 2014. www.washingtonpost.com

Thomas, C., My Granfather's Son: A Memoir. © HarperCollins publishers. 2007. www.HarperCollins.com

Thompson, N. *Ricardian socialists/Smithian socialists: what's in a name.* © Cambridge University Press. 2010

Western Goals Foundation. *No Place to Hide: The Strategy and Tactics of Terrorism"* documentary. November 2, 2010.